What Is Church?

C_{hurch?}

What Is Church?

A Story of Transition

Mike Bishop

Foreword by Todd Hunter

Missio Dei Publishing

What Is Church? A Story of Transition

Missio Dei Publishing

Published by
Missio Dei Publishing
An Imprint of Harmon Press
Woodinville, WA 98077
http://www.harmonpress.com

ISBN-10: 0-9799076-3-2
ISBN-13: 978-0-9799076-3-0

Library of Congress Control Number: 2008942325

All Scripture quotations, unless otherwise noted, are taken from
The New International Version of the Bible, © 1975, 1978, 1984 by
International Bible Society.

Cover Concept by: Mike Bishop
Cover Design by: Harmon Press

What Is Church?

Contents

What Is Church?

What Is Church?

Foreword
Todd Hunter

I met Mike Bishop near the turn of this last century. You may remember the times. We had somehow made it through the gigantic scare of all our computers and related technology crashing in 2000 and 9/11 was on all our minds and hearts. In addition, for those of us who work with the church, things that no one would have ever questioned even a few years earlier were now open to discussion among reasonable and devoted Christians.

For the church, this evolution began a few years before the year 2000 when a few new words crept into our vocabulary: postmodernism and post-Christendom to mention just two. It is remarkable how much power some words have. Some give great comfort—*mom* or *grace*. Others strike so much fear they can give sensitive people

1

What Is Church?

panic attacks—*earthquake* or *test*. The *post* words of the late twentieth and early twenty-first centuries upset much of the church. I know; I lived through it and heard the debates from the best thinkers on all sides of the issues.

To my surprise and relief, I found in Mike Bishop and his colleagues all over America something different than mere skeptical hand wringing. They were conversant with all the debates, but they were not that interested—just marginally so. Their real focus was on these questions: What do we do about what we know? How do we faithfully follow Jesus and proclaim the good news of the Gospel of the Kingdom in a culture that is genuinely changing right under our feet?

Let's stop here for a moment—let me back up and tell you how I bumped into Mike. From 1994 to 2001, I was National Coordinator/Director of Vineyard Churches USA. Though I love and respect the Vineyard and have great relationships within it, I resigned my position to *get back into the game* of evangelistic church planting. I have always loved evangelism. Billy Graham and Greg Laurie were my earliest heroes and I even tried crusade type evangelism. I was okay at it, but over time and through frustration I learned that I was no Greg or Billy. Thus, over the years of my life, I have mostly expressed my passion for evangelism through planting churches that were designed expressly to make new followers, new disciples of Jesus.

A few weeks after I resigned, a young man named Mark Priddy asked to come to Anaheim to see me. I had spoken to him once before on the phone and something inside told me to meet with him. As he sat down in my office, he told me his story—his love for the Kingdom, his love for the Vineyard and John Wimber, the successful business he had recently sold, and his vision to help young leaders like himself figure out how to navigate the churning waters of our shifting culture. His idea was to start a ministry that would coach young leaders. We made a deal pretty quickly. I cannot remember if it was that day or not, but we were rapidly on the same page. Mark created an organization called Allelon and hired me to be its first church planting coach.

At the time, I lived in Yorba Linda, California—a neighboring city to Anaheim. I rented a small office from a friend who was a lawyer. When I say *small*, I really mean a closet that doubled as a storage and copier room. I literally worked in a 3 foot by 5 foot space and loved every minute of it. Those couple years were some of the most rewarding of my life. Most days I had back to back phone appointments like a doctor or a therapist, sitting with a headset on eight to ten hours a day learning from people like Mike. They thought I was teaching and mentoring them, but in hindsight I think I may have learned more from them as they opened their hearts, minds, and souls.

Mike picks up the story in the pages ahead. As you turn the page and begin to read, I want you to know that I really admire what Mike and his friends are tying to do. They do not need to get everything right for me to respect them. We need risk takers—people who get some things wrong, which allow others to build on their mistakes. There is no such thing as context-less evangelism. Contexts change, that means we must change. Change requires risk—and I admire those who take such risks.

You will surely not agree with all the conclusions to which Mike has come, but that is not important. I commend *What is Church?* to you because I know you will grow reading it in the same manner I grew through living the story with Mike and his friends.

—Todd Hunter ✦ August 2008 ✦ Eagle, ID

Introduction

It's time. It's time to lay aside timidity, to push through the fear. It's time to grab a hold of the confidence, to blow up the excuses. It's time to do all of the things that you have dreamed of doing. There is nothing holding you back except yourself.

I felt a surge of excitement in that—a shift in my attitude, my countenance was lifted, my head was raised. This was more than "the giant within" Tony Robbins-speak. This was more than positive thinking. I sensed that this was the Counselor, the only one who can empower me to accomplish all that I've dreamed.

I'm not going to apologize for sharing this, though the enemy of my soul wants me to. There is a latent creative force in every human being that is groaning to be released.

Thirty-four is not the time to stifle it. Neither is four or 104.

It's time.

For me. And, I dare say, it's time for you.

Chad Canipe wrote these words in May of 2005. He had just turned thirty-four, the age I am about to turn in a month. Chad wanted to plant a church in Norwood, an off-the-beaten-path section of Cincinnati, a place he lived with his wife and two sons, a place he loved. He did not care too much for the typical church planting methodologies. He loved people. He loved the city. He wanted to see city people formed into disciples of Jesus, into people who loved God and neighbor. He was going to spend the rest of his life giving himself towards this end, towards God's kingdom.

Chad died on March 10, 2006.

But Chad was not alone in his dream. Far from it.

A few weeks later, Mark Palmer died after a long battle with cancer. Mark lived in Columbus, Ohio, with his wife and son. He too carried Chad's dream in his heart and was living it out with a ragtag group of college students and misfits of the city. That community of faith, The Landing Place, is still there, still carrying the dream.

They are not alone either. Far from it.

What Is Church?

The purpose of this book is not to try to answer that question in an academic sense. Nor is it an attempt to present a model for *doing church* to prop up along side the other models in the Christian marketplace. This is not a *how-to* or *why* book, but simply offers this question for your consideration: What if? What if the dream Chad Canipe and

What Is Church?

Mark Palmer carried around with them expressed something profound about the heart of God for the church in America and the world? What if there are echoes of their dream popping up literally everywhere, but not necessarily in the places you might expect?

In 2001, the former National Director of the Association of Vineyard Churches, Todd Hunter, began mentoring a group of young church planters. I was one of those church planters, as was Mark Palmer and many other friends of mine. We did not know each other at the time and our church backgrounds were quite different. One of the things Todd helped us do was learn how to ask questions, the right questions. We were all preparing to be leaders, not of religious organizations per se, but of what we were first beginning to call *missional communities*. Many of us had been very successful as ministry leaders in church before. Youth pastors. Worship leaders. Teaching pastors. Leaders of small group ministries. However, in our own ways there were two things we felt were supremely lacking in our experience of church up until that point: we wanted deeper relationship with fellow disciples of Jesus and we wanted desperately to discover and join in on God's mission to the world. Todd was helping us verbalize the questions we needed to ask if that desire was to become a reality. We all had our own lists, but the ones Todd and myself talked about most looked like this:

✦ What is church? (Or what did Jesus intend his church to be?)
✦ What does it mean to be a follower of Jesus? (Or what does it mean to be an authentic Christian?)
✦ What is the gospel Jesus preached?
✦ What does it mean to be authentically spiritual (In light of cultural definitions of *spiritual*)?
✦ What does it mean to be a leader in Jesus' church?

What Is Church?

We discovered that questions such as these have been asked throughout church history. However, the answers to these questions were not going to come quickly or resolutely. We would have to work out answers in community, over a long period of time, with the witness of Scripture and God's people through the centuries as our guides. Throw out the typical church planting timeline. Trash the two-year-plans and marketing campaigns. This was more like the work of jungle missionaries. Break out the compass and map; all of us were suddenly in vastly unfamiliar territory.

Slowly, these little missional communities began to pop up all over the country. You have never heard of them and in the beginning most of us truly thought we were the only ones who were asking these kinds of questions. My wife Amber and I began meeting with two other couples in our hometown of Jupiter, Florida. There were groups in places like Cincinnati, Lexington, Southern California, and Michigan. We spent a lot of our early time as communities trying to make sense of things and learning how to love each other without most of the trappings of church. There were plenty of struggles. Some of us faced pressure from denominations and their leaders. Some worked multiple jobs because their only experience was in professional ministry. Others simply had trouble finding people who had similar concerns about church and a desire for authentic community. We often felt completely alone. We wondered what we were doing. We questioned whether God was really in this thing we had gotten ourselves into.

So many of us started writing, blogging, to be more precise. And pretty quickly we found each other.

This is our story.

Break out the compass and map...

What Is Church?

We Are Misfits

American culture has a love/hate relationship with misfits. We enjoy watching amateur singers on television make fools of themselves. We cheer when the unexpected college basketball team reaches the Final Four. We make celebrities out of the little guys who make us laugh, win the lottery, or beat the odds in some other way. But we find it difficult to imagine that we might be misfits ourselves. After all, misfits do not often become heroes, and they typically do not remain heroes for long.

This book is written for a certain kind of misfit, many who are just recognizing that not fitting in is more normal than they thought. They belong to a group of human beings who have a long history of not being able to square with the status quo. In fact, the Founder of their movement seemed to relish the fact that most of the words that came out of his mouth did not make much sense to the general population. Yet somehow, in spite of the mystery and unpopularity of his words, there have been groups of people ever since who have put his words into practice, into life.

Christianity is fundamentally a religion to be lived. This does not make it unique in the world of religions, but it does challenge a growing segment of religious culture in America that desires deeper spirituality. Christians seem to have a knack for putting flesh and blood on their faith, for good or ill. This is in part because of their stubborn belief that Jesus was a flesh and blood human being, commonly known as *incarnation*. Jesus was born, lived, and died on the same earth on which we still plant farms, build cities, and raise children. His world carried with it the same elements of humanity we try to manage in our world. He lived as most of the population of our world lives today—poor. Jesus had none of the privileges of wealth or birthright, so he spent an inordinate amount of time surviving. Within that context of anonymous survival, his ministry began. Soon he had gathered around himself a small group of survivors, men and women who had a variety of motives for being with him. Regardless, their common bond was that Jesus was someone they could *follow*. They were tired of the false piety and political maneuvering of the people who claimed to be their leaders. Most of them were trying to live righteously, or were at least trying to imagine themselves as something other than a sinner. These survivors needed someone they could get their hands on and hear his voice. When Jesus came along and said, "Follow me," they did not think, "Here is my next spiritual guru!" No, they *followed* him, and left nothing behind.

Christians have historically given this idea of lived religion a name—discipleship. In our culture, a disciple is someone who has studied under a famous researcher or professor, or an athlete who has mastered his or her sport under the tutelage of a hall-of-fame coach. But a disciple could also be someone who has read every book by a motivational speaker and attends all of her conferences. That reading and listening implies dedication, but not necessarily discipleship. To be a disciple of Jesus is a very serious thing if you read the gospels. He, in fact, seemed less concerned with his disciples actually understanding what he said and did. Rather, he wanted them to be attentive to *how* he said and did things, to learn his rhythm, his moves. Jesus knew he was modeling life, not just teaching ideas about God, so the real challenge for his disciples went far beyond buying into his particular interpretation of scripture or commentary on the future of the Jewish people. The challenge, his narrow path, was if they would leave "... home or brothers or sisters or mother or father or children or fields for me and the gospel" (Mark 10.29). The seriousness of his call to discipleship cannot be understated.

What Is Church?

The god of individualism in our culture makes it difficult for us to conceive what it might look like to actually follow a physical Jesus. If he showed up at your doorstep or at your office and said, "Follow me," with no qualification, he would probably get the same response we give most door-to-door salespeople. As Americans, we will protect our autonomy—with violence if necessary—even though we may freely give our allegiance to God, country, and other causes. However, Jesus did not ask his followers for their allegiance or their vote. His call went right to the heart of the matter. Who is your god? Who gets the final word in the way you live your life? *Follow me* punctures all that we manufacture as spirituality or religion like a child's balloon. We stand there, our nets in hand, at the tax-collecting table, at the grocery store, in our cars, at our jobs, with our families, in our neighborhoods...and he waits for us to decide.

In the next chapter, I will talk about the context necessary to understand how discipleship to Jesus is possible in our culture: the Kingdom of God. Without a kingdom context, asking a question like "What is church?" might simply be the wrong question. In Chapters Two, Three, and Four, I will describe the transition many of us have gone through as church planters and followers of Jesus. Although much of what I will describe relates to my personal story, what I have experienced is by no means unique. For many who read this book, you will probably hear echoes of your own story throughout those chapters. The rest of the book is an attempt to spark your imagination to begin exploring the "What if?" question I posed earlier. It is not meant to be an exhaustive or authoritative study on church structure or, on the other hand, something akin to *Church for Dummies* filled with pragmatism. Walter Brueggemann communicates the kind of provocation helpful to the task at hand:

What Is Church?

The prophet does not ask if the vision can be implemented, for questions of implementation are of no consequence until the vision can be imagined. The imagination must come before the implementation. Our culture is competent to implement almost anything and to imagine almost nothing.[1]

The Webster's definition of *implementation* is "to give practical effect to and ensure of actual fulfillment by concrete measures." Practical. Concrete. Our culture certainly has the competence to accomplish many a practical and concrete objective. But *imagination* takes time, space, dare I say... leisure. I have three young children who occasionally rely on their father to prepare dinner. Have you ever tried to prepare a creative meal while three hungry, tired children are in the kitchen waiting for their plates? Imaginative cooking is not an option at that point I'm afraid.

Imagination confronts the tendency to rapidly build something new on sand rather than take the time to find solid rock. Extreme patience is required, something implementers typically do not have in abundance. However, it is my experience that what looks like wasting time to an implementer, might in fact be the very thing God uses to form you into what he desires, and then places you into the very center of what he is doing.

Criticism vs. Critique

It would be helpful at this point to establish a few assumptions and generally set the stage so this book can be placed in its proper context. First of all, I am a Christian; someone who has placed my hope in Jesus of Nazareth to be saved not only from myself, but from everything our world considers *the good life*. The hope of heaven is the understanding that Jesus is about his Father's business of setting things right in the world. This is his work, his dream, as King. As his people, we have the choice to be about the Father's business as well, or we can attempt ill-advised side ventures. Sticking with the Father's business is usually best.

You will not hear much discussion in this book regarding the emerging church, as it is becoming commonly known, or related organizations such as Emergent Village. If you are searching for a study on what is being described as the emerging church, let me suggest you read *Emerging Churches: Creating Christian Community in Postmodern Cultures* by Eddie Gibbs and Ryan K. Bolger. Their study is fair, comprehensive, and deals with actual practitioners who have started churches who might classify themselves as emerging. Some of the groups represented in this book are also described in Gibbs and Bolger's book; however, this is fundamentally not a study on what the emerging church is or is not. Frankly, there are plenty of controversies surrounding the emerging church that are unique to American Christianity. What God is doing in his kingdom all over the world transcends many of these controversies. This global phenomenon of the church in transition is closer to what I would classify as the real emerging church.

You will also not hear much in this book about postmodernism, if you are familiar with the term. Not that understanding what the impact of postmodernity has had on our culture is unimportant, it is just a little like snorkeling through a coral reef teeming with brilliant tropical sea life, and then describing to your friends back on shore the attributes of the water. Postmodernity is the water we swim in, whether we like it or not. It does not have to control us, although we would be foolish to close our eyes and pretend it is not there. To carry the snorkeling metaphor a little further (but hopefully not too far), the clear, tropical ocean water supports an entirely different ecosystem than that on land or in fresh water. If the chemical makeup of the water were to change even slightly, the ecosystem would be destroyed. Those plants and animals were built to live in that water; it was God's intention that they live there and only there. For the swimmer, if he or she ignores the water there could be equally deadly consequences. Disciples of Jesus understand that living in a postmodern world is inevitable. It surrounds us, but it is not our home.

Just as context is vital to understanding culture, so it is when trying to describe the eureka moments of transition. Along with the "What if?" questions that this book will pose, there will naturally be portraits of what already is to provide contrast. To those still heavily invested in particular ideas of church, those contrasts may seem overly critical, generalized, and perhaps unnecessary. It is not my intention to criticize for criticism's sake—to throw stones at the proverbial glass house—but rather to create some space for fresh ideas, for imagination to flourish. In the English language, a word that may be better suited to describe this would be *critique*. Transition, change of any sort, requires a bit of detachment in order to fully comprehend what is worth changing and what is worth keeping.

The next assumption I want to establish deals with the kind of men and women who will hopefully find this book helpful. In the past five years, I have met many people who love Jesus but are dying in church. They are not what I would describe as bitter or angry, although if you heard some of their stories, you might not blame them for being a little disturbed. Most of them have been Christians for many years, others for only a short time. They have been faithful to serve the church in every capacity, some as full-time employees and others with literally almost all their spare time. They have given tremendous sums of money, provided their professional expertise at little or no cost, opened their homes, sacrificed their weekends, used up their vacation time, and invested in difficult and often painful relationships with other church members. However, at the end of the day, these men and women look at the work of their hands and wonder, is this what God created me for, *us* for? They feel deeply as if something is wrong, yet do not wish to hurt the feelings of those other servants around them who seem to receive so much joy out of their service. They wonder, "Am I the problem? Maybe I should just keep my mouth shut and not rock the boat." But that nagging feeling will not go away. "Surely there is more to church than putting on a good Sunday service. Surely there is more to evangelism than passing out a tract or hosting a Christian rock concert. Surely there is more to studying the Bible together than listening to a sermon once or twice a week in the same room or filling out a workbook. Surely there is more to being a pastor than preaching a good one once in a while and making sure there are enough people in the back to hand out bulletins. Surely, I am not the only one wondering about these things."

You are not alone. Whether you are a pastor or preschool worker, worship leader or window washer, you were created to be God's unique children, his special people. Finding your *purpose* does not mean you identify your place in someone else's dream. Rather, it is a process of discovery that may bring you to a place of culturally disapproved ends. Along the way, it is critical to have friends, fathers, and mothers around you, all of which are difficult to come by. It is my hope that books such as this one become rallying points to help you find friends and mentors for your own journey. There is really no other way we can move forward as God's people.

Finally, and there is no polite way to say this, if you are

looking for advice on how to plant the next great American church, this might not be the book for you. This is also not a source for fresh ideas about how to start house churches or a guide to starting an emerging church. This is plain and simple not a book for entrepreneurs, but for people of no reputation. Gordon Cosby was the founder of The Church of the Savior in Washington D.C., a group I will explain in more detail later. Church of the Savior has been know for its incredible impact on one neighborhood in D.C. and has influenced thousands of people in their sixty years as a community of faith. Cosby once was invited to speak to a group of megachurch pastors who expected him to lecture on how he was able to create an environment where so much remarkable ministry happened among such a relatively small group of people. The title of Cosby's speech to these men was, "Vision, the Destroyer of Essence." Ouch.

We are a culture that worships the visionary leader and entrepreneurial spirit. What Gordon Cosby understood is that vision can become an enemy to true health, to authentic success. The essence that we seek is more mysterious than we would like to admit. Intuitively we know we cannot simply recreate the early church we find in the book of Acts, but we make attempts regardless. The essence of church is found within unique, anonymous groups of *people*, not in trying to recreate some first century ideal or by creating a superior brand to market to Christian consumers. The stories you will read throughout the rest of this book are representative of these kinds of groups, made up of imperfect, non-heroic people. Their source, their raison d'être, is the kingdom of God. It is to the kingdom that we must turn our attention next.

Chapter One

Entering the Dream of God

Growing up evangelical, I was no stranger to the altar call. How many times did I hear the words, "With every head bowed and eye closed, slip up your hand if you want to give your life to Jesus?" Those that took the plunge were then admonished to make the trek down front to say the sinner's prayer. Afterwards, they were given a Bible, told to attend the church, and basically be thankful because *now you will be going to heaven when you die.*

At some point in my experience I began to question why there was so much emphasis on getting people to *say the prayer*. The nagging thought, which so many of my friends seemed to pass over all too easily, was *What happened next?* What happened to these countless souls who had seemingly passed from death to life? What were the means to becoming the kind of people that the Bible indicated as normal Christian experience? For me, reading passages like the Sermon on the Mount, or Romans 8 or 12, or Ephesians 6 were more than a little disconcerting. They seemed to paint the picture of a person whose entire life was directed by a source far outside the central processing unit most people carry around in their bodies. The Sermon on the Mount, which you might like to call the Kingdom Manifesto, reads more like something you would find on hacker's website. Following Jesus or breaking into mainframes cannot be done in three easy steps. There is a language to learn, a culture to adopt, an *attitude* that becomes your modus operandi. As in hacking, perhaps the goal of the gospel is not always about *getting in*.

There were answers to my questions, but none of them seemed very satisfactory. People talked about discipleship, but it seemed far secondary to preparing souls for heaven. Discipleship required the hard work of walking with a person through something akin to an exilic return. This journey was fraught with danger, questions, and pain, which any practical ideas on discipleship I encountered seemed ill equipped to manage. For the most part, new believers were left to fend for themselves outside the time they spent in meetings and programmed times.

This bothered me greatly, because in part *I did not know how to fend for myself*. I had learned how to create a comfortable life within the church and had developed quite a detailed apologetic for why that sheltered existence was not only beneficial to me, but was *God's will*. I had no tools for helping actual people experience a personal exodus into the kingdom of God. My ministry was a paper tiger, adept at things like leading a small group discussion and knowing how to structure a worship set to produce the desired effect. But when it came to entering the mess of a human life battered by sin, I had only the latest program or technique at my disposal. If that person did not fit in my program, I was at a loss for words.

Dallas Willard calls discipleship the "elephant in the church."[1] An enormous, messy elephant is walking around in our living room and we act like it doesn't exist. My journey began by confronting this elephant head on. I wanted to be a part of a faith community that refused to gloss over the bare, naked facts. We would, in fact, center ourselves around the question of "What is next?" If heaven truly is the reign of God in its fulfillment, then I wanted to begin experiencing a little of heaven on earth now. And not just on Sunday and Wednesday nights either, but at my job, in my home, with my friends, and in the quiet spaces.

...discipleship the elephant in the church.

Over the past few years there has been much written about the gospel being something larger than what we have known in evangelical circles. It is not my intention to repeat here the work already done, but to show how this gospel influences actual followers of Jesus in community for the sake of the world. One of my first exposures to this message was through the founder of the Association of Vineyard Churches, John Wimber, and his theological mentor, George Eldon Ladd. Later, my understanding deepened through books like *The Divine Conspiracy* by Dallas Willard, *Missional Church* edited by Darrel Guder, and *The Challenge of Jesus* by N. T. Wright. These pastors and theologians have become my guides in this new world/old world of the gospel. There are many older, wiser men and women who have come before, but these individuals have been speaking the loudest to me in my generation.

What Is Church?

The Gospel of the Kingdom

> After John was put in prison, Jesus went into
> Galilee, proclaiming the good news of God. "The
> time has come," he said. "The kingdom of God is
> near. Repent and believe the good news!"
> (Mark 1.14–15)

Most average Bible readers probably read over the
first few paragraphs of Mark without a lot of meditation.
It is early in the book, which we often think of as passive,
introductory matters. But these were Romans that Mark was
writing to and they were not people known for their patience.
They were action junkies, probably much like twenty-first
century Americans. Read how Mark begins his gospel: *The
beginning of the gospel about Jesus Christ, the Son of God.* No fancy
prologue here about angels, wise men, and a little boy wowing
priests in the temple. He jumps straight to the meat of the
story—*who* was this Jesus and what did he come to do?

The first time I heard Mark 1.15 in a sermon, it
thoroughly took me off-guard. Todd Hunter was giving a
short message to a group of students at a regional Vineyard
pastor's conference soon after he had resigned as National
Director in 2000. He began the message with the words,
"Tonight I'm going to explain life to you." That will get
anyone's attention, even a group of disaffected pastor's kids.
He then read Mark 1.14 and 15 and asked if it sounded like
any gospel presentation they had ever heard, "Jesus went into
Galilee, proclaiming the good news of God...the kingdom
of God is near." So what is this kingdom, and why is it good
news that it is near? Where is the cross, the body and blood,
the resurrection, atonement, forgiveness, redemption, I
thought this was supposed to be the *gospel?*

What Is Church?

If you have not figured this out yet, evangelicals have a bad habit of reducing enormous theological landscapes into principles or spiritual laws. On the other hand, we have been just as guilty of making simple things extremely complicated. In this case, I am walking on the thin ice of making both mistakes at once. How do I describe the beauty and intricacy of the message of the kingdom that Jesus preached that simultaneously re-orients *and* deciphers everything about the question, "What is the gospel?" But at the same time, how do I become a convincing witness that the gospel of the kingdom is nothing new or novel, requires no secret knowledge or funky exegetical manipulation, and would make sense to a five-year old? Here is the truth: I cannot. To this end, I must again defer to those who are much wiser and more learned than myself and can walk the thin ice without taking a dive. That being said, I cannot ignore the fact that Jesus' message of the kingdom is, literally and figuratively, the crux of everything this book represents. Without the kingdom, this would simply be another book about *doing church differently* that is becoming so nauseatingly commonplace. If you are wondering about church but do not have a kingdom context, your journey will most likely end in disappointment and disillusionment.

First, it is important to define clearly what the kingdom of God is before understanding how it impacts our view of church. The kingdom is simply the rule or reign of God. Willard describes the kingdom in this way:

> God's own 'kingdom' or 'rule' is the range of his effective will, where what he wants done is done. The person of God himself and the action of his will are the organizing principles of his kingdom, but everything that obeys those principles, whether by nature or by choice, is within his kingdom.[2]

Obviously, when words such as *rule* or *reign* are

mentioned, we begin to think about the political arena. Who really has power? How is that power distributed? If power is being used in a destructive way, how is that power overthrown? The first century Jewish people were clearly frustrated with both the rule of Rome and the local rule of Herod and the chief priests. The options lain before them were familiar ones: fight, compromise, or run away. Entire communities of Jews formed around each of these responses,[3] but none of them were successful in overthrowing the kingdoms in power. In this highly charged atmosphere, Jesus comes along announcing that the kingdom of God was near. To first century ears, that announcement would be filtered through the three options. Was he saying it was time to pick up arms and overthrow the Romans with God's help? Was God saying they should side with the Romans and other ruling parties and seek some sort of peaceful coexistence? Or, was God calling them to leave Jerusalem and form utopian communities away from civilization? Jesus did not answer those questions right away, but rather *acted* in a manner that demonstrated an entirely new option, an option centered around himself.

Jesus began his ministry by calling twelve (an auspicious number by Jewish standards) radically different men to leave their homes, jobs, and families to follow him. He was not forming a brute squad or a team of servants, but rather, a representative people. This ragtag group would be joined by the flotsam and jetsam of the Jewish countryside as Jesus began to travel around announcing his kingdom message. N.T. Wright describes Jesus' intentions in this way:

> The key thing was that the inbreaking kingdom Jesus was announcing created a new world, a new context, and he was challenging his hearers to become the new people that this new context demanded, the citizens of this new world. He was offering a challenge to his

contemporaries to a way of life, a way of forgiveness and prayer, a way of jubilee, which they could practice in their own villages, right where they were.[3]

The new world Jesus introduced involved neither violence, compromise, or escape. "If someone strikes you on the right cheek, turn to him the other also" (Matthew 5.39b). "But seek first his kingdom and his righteousness, and all these things will be given to you as well" (Matthew 6.33). "You are the light of the world. A city on a hill cannot be hidden" (Matthew 5.14). This world was going to come alive literally right in front of their noses. The incarnation of Jesus is not an abstract theological idea to be argued among scholars while debating his divinity. "The Word became flesh and blood, and moved into the neighborhood." (John 1.14a, *The Message*). The incarnation is representative of this new kingdom reality and its accessibility. God is on the scene. For a first century Jew, if you let your imagination run a bit and think back to your knowledge of the Hebrew scriptures, this is incredibly *good news.*

Forgiveness. Justice. Mercy. Healing. Sacrifice. Peace. Wholeness. Community. Power. Life. Light. Resurrection. The themes of the New Testament begin to take on a whole new reality. This stuff is really livable, by everyday average people no less. Preparing souls for heaven seems to pale in comparison to introducing people to this *way of life.* Willard helps us begin to understand what this might mean in twenty-first century America:

> Jesus came among us to show and teach the life for which we were made. He came very gently, opened access to the governance of God with him, and set afoot a conspiracy of freedom in truth among human beings. Having overcome death he remains among us. By relying on his word and presence we are enabled

to reintegrate the little realm that makes up our life
into the infinite rule of God. And that is the eternal
kind of life. Caught up in his active rule, our deeds
become an element in God's eternal history. They are
what God and we do together, making us part of his
life and him a part of ours.[6]

For twenty centuries, God's people have in one form or
another demonstrated the eternal kind of life to the world.
It has not always been pretty, but God never seems to give
up looking for those who will join his redemptive project.
In our day, he is again searching for a people who will call
him, and him alone, King.

The Greatest Show on Earth

The American hunger for drama is insatiable. In 2004,
Americans spent $40.6 billion on video rentals and sales
combined, not to mention the $8.75 billion spent at the
box office.[7] In that same year, Mel Gibson's film, *The Passion
of the Christ*, stormed into the focus of popular culture and
the church. The film generated $370 million and a flood of
endless controversy. Church leaders seized the opportunity
to ride the wave by buying out whole theaters for the opening
weekend in order for Christians to invite their non-believing
friends. The film faithfully depicted, in graphic, gruesome
detail, the events of Jesus' last twenty-four hours. People
of all religious and social backgrounds were left weeping in
their comfortable theater seats. The stark reality of what
Jesus endured in those hours was impossible to ignore or
walk away from quickly. Yet in spite of what the movie
accomplished, later that year the country endured one of
the most bitterly contested and polarizing presidential
elections on record. The media segregated us into *red* or *blue*
depending on our political affiliations. Both sides spewed

What Is Church?

venom that encouraged the divisions to grow deeper and in some cases sparked violence. Hardly the reconciliation Jesus preached or Mel Gibson hoped to bring.

The message of the kingdom says that the drama we are searching for is far more real than our favorite reality show on television. In fact, this drama is open to anyone who wants to participate, no acting experience necessary. Wright gives us a starting place for joining the troupe:

> When Jesus announced the kingdom, the stories he told functioned like dramatic plays in search of actors. His hearers where invited to audition for parts in the kingdom. They had been eager for God's drama to be staged and were waiting to find out what they would have to do when he did so. Now they were to discover. They were to become kingdom-people themselves. Jesus, following John the Baptist, was calling into being what he believed would be the true, renewed people of God.[8]

Entering God's kingdom is like running off to join the circus, the Greatest Show on Earth, but then finding out that the circus is going to stay permanently in your hometown, right on your doorstep. This is an uncomfortable realization for the American church. The gospel we are used to centers on two things: preparing for the rapture and getting into heaven if you happen to die first. Matters of how we go about living our lives now, about *discipleship*, are secondary and in some cases, optional. It is not until we become acquainted with this kingdom message, understand how it was heard in the first century by Jewish ears, and see how the rest of the New Testament makes sense in light of it, do we begin to see how immediate the gospel really is. The hope we have is not because we get to escape the world, but rather that we can understand the way the world is really supposed to work and live in it accordingly.

Again, if you desire to understand more about God's

kingdom, there are many faithful guides available for your quest, and they come from all corners of the church. George Eldon Ladd was a professor of theology at Fuller Seminary and wrote extensively on the kingdom. N.T. Wright is an Anglican Bishop and historian whose work on the historical Jesus and the early church is as accessible as it is compelling. Dallas Willard is a Southern Baptist and professor of philosophy at USC who writes and teaches on the kingdom and implementing the teachings of Jesus in our real lives. There are many others I could list, however, the task before us now is asking how the kingdom of God provides a proper context for the questions I posed back in the introduction:

- ✦ What is church? (Or what did Jesus intend his church to be?)
- ✦ What does it mean to be a follower of Jesus? (Or what does it mean to be an authentic Christian?)
- ✦ What is the gospel Jesus preached?
- ✦ What does it mean to be authentically spiritual (In light of cultural definitions of *spiritual*)?
- ✦ What does it mean to be a leader in Jesus' church?

It might be helpful to first show what answering those questions *without* a kingdom context might look like. First of all, *church* in all its forms, has become something which entirely too much time and energy is spent fussing over. Beyond the sheer number of denominational varieties, there are exponentially more methodologies of how a church should be *run*. We talk about *doing church* in much the same way we talk about *doing business* or *doing family*. There are, obviously, countless ways to run a business or have a family and opinions about those ways run passionately deep. In relationship to church, we add to the mix what we believe to be an ancient, authoritative text—the Bible—that supposedly is giving us a framework for all of our church-related doing. We debate the intricacies of the words within, which often translate into new methodologies or sub-groups of sub-groups of sub-groups. Buried in the debate, there is a longing to get past the politics and idealism and simply have a church Jesus would be proud of. Yet, what typically happens appears to be distraction on a colossal scale. We are distracted by our doctrinal differences. We are distracted by our building projects. We are distracted by our latest attempts to satisfy the average American's hunger for drama.

In the midst of all this diversion, it is easy to see how we could miss the simplicity of Jesus' message. Drowned out by the noise is a lone voice saying, "Follow me." Occasionally, in the unanticipated quiet spaces of our lives, we hear this voice calling, but we typically do not know how to respond. Instead, we are fed more sermons, more workbooks, more prayers to pray, more ministries to serve in, more *spiritual technology* to improve our lives. We begin to equate our service to God with our service to a political party or a cultural ideal. Why bother with the words of Jesus when the American Dream is doing us just fine? But when that dream fails us, we turn again to our god-technology for another attempt at satiation.

So what was Jesus' message to the world? There are those who would have us believe that the gospel is predominantly about Jesus fixing our individual sin problem so that we can go to heaven when we die. There are others who are obsessed with Jesus' message of good news to the poor and commitment to *the least of these*. There are still others who want to remake Jesus into a sage of life, an old guru with fresh things to say to the twenty-first century world about spirituality, leadership, war, or justice.

In the face of these competing visions of Jesus, many people in and out of the church are either confused or convinced (to the point of violence) of their own minority position. The rest are left with just trying to be as *spiritual* as possible. Becoming religious is a slippery slope. After all, the terrorists of 9/11 were doing everything in the name of their religious beliefs. Jesusy-spirituality allows us to keep our political affiliations intact, our standard of living stable, our friends friends, and our enemies enemies, but all the while get a little help on the side making it through this ugly world. Modern Christian Spirituality is not as cool as being a Buddhist or devotee of Kaballah, but if you keep quiet about it, people will respect you for your *faith*. Get too loud or opinionated and you will find yourself aligned with the Pat Robertsons and Jerry Falwells of the world—definitely not cool. The safe thing is to go to church on Sundays, read your Bible once in awhile, pray at family meals, and try to not overtly screw anyone at work. Oh yeah, and if anyone asks, never tell them you voted for George W. Bush.

In the middle of this cultural Christian morass stands the professional minister. Years of seminary or Bible school could never have prepared him or her for interpreting these realities. Yet, somehow, thousands of ministers are paid to do just that. What does it mean to be a leader in Jesus' church? Models abound. There is the visionary corporate CEO, mobilizing vast resources, money, and people, to reach more of the world for Jesus. There is the passionate motivational speaker, cajoling his or her flocks to get on board with enthusiasm for the successful life God intends. There is the prophetic voice in the wilderness, clamoring to call attention to a social disease and rallying every available resource towards its healing. Obviously, ministers find varying levels of success, whatever your definition of success might be, with these and other models of leadership. In the vacuum of success are those who are either burned out or feel totally inadequate to the task. Others redefine the rules altogether and provide whatever spiritual services the market demands. Or, taking an ever popular solution, the cultural realities are simply ignored in favor of creating a social ideal that revolves around religious traditions.

The kingdom of God presents a reality, centered on the person of Jesus and everything he was and is; that directly confronts our culture's answers to the questions above. The people who answer his call to become apprenticed to him in the kingdom will simply defy category. They will seem annoyingly unconcerned with church politics or organizational methods, and will choose to associate with all the wrong people. They will not rely on spiritual technology to *get fed*, but will identify God's presence in all sorts of places and seem quite content with very little. The culture will see them as cool in some aspects and quite disconcerting in others. And as they begin to form little fellowships of other disciples, their understanding of leadership will probably come from sources like *The Lord of the Rings* rather than *The 21 Irrefutable Laws of Leadership*.

Without going into much more detail, you are hopefully beginning to recognize that the transition before us as American Christians is a daunting one. Total loss is not only possible; it is expected. Put yourself in the shoes of a first-century Jew for a second. Imagine living your entire life with the understanding that God's saving presence on earth only resides in the temple of Jerusalem, which has now been bastardized by Herod and his quest for power. Along comes Jesus, a no-body carpenter from no-where Nazareth, who announces in word and deed that God's presence, power, and authority is now free and available everywhere. What would it take to believe him? What would it take to follow him? What would you have to let go of? The transition we face now is perhaps not as challenging as the one those people of Palestine confronted, but that does not mean it will be easy. In business speak, a paradigm shift of massive proportions is necessary in order to really see the kingdom of God in this time. Personally, my experience looked more like going through detox.

Chapter Two
Detoxing from Church

By then I wasn't just asking questions; I was being changed by them. I was being changed by my prayers, which dwindled down nearer and nearer to silence, which weren't confrontations with God but with the difficulty—in my own mind, or in the human lot—of knowing what or how to pray. Lying awake at night, I could feel myself being changed—into what, I had no idea. It was worse than wondering if I had received the call. I wasn't just a student or a going-to-be-preacher anymore. I was a lost traveler wandering in the woods, needing to be on my way somewhere but not knowing where.[1]

In 1998, I was living the life of an evangelical poster-child. After graduating from the University of Florida in

What Is Church?

1996, my primary occupation was working as an industrial engineer for a large battery manufacturing plant. This is what paid the bills and where I lived forty-hours-a-week. However, I was also an at-a-distance student of the Vineyard Leadership Institute (VLI) preparing to become a church planter to be sent from a Vineyard church in Gainesville, Florida. Somewhere in the few waking hours that remained I led a small group, led worship once a month, oversaw the multimedia ministry, and tried to maintain my marriage. Real life was rushing from work to dinner to small group and then home to study for a few hours before bed. Real life was full of quick, desperate prayers to move me from point A to point B. Real life was wishing I could get up to read my Bible at 6:30 before the commute to work, but instead, waking up at eight, grabbing a bagel, and running out the door sipping coffee.

At that point in my life, I had been a Christian for twenty years. I had experienced the mystery of God in a Lutheran church, the power of God in a Charismatic church, the relevance of worship and scripture in a Calvary Chapel, and the call to evangelism in Campus Crusade for Christ. The tribe I had settled in, the Vineyard, was a place where these diverse streams seemed to flow into a contiguous river. God had called me into *full-time ministry* and I was pursuing that call through whatever means necessary. In VLI, I was learning to be a leader, a theologian, and a pastor. But I hadn't banked on what I was about to learn next.

I was taking a class entitled "The Leader's Spiritual Formation." It was a pretty straightforward class, primarily about the spiritual disciplines: prayer, fasting, study, worship, and some disciplines that seemed foreign to my evangelical ears. I had always felt like a failure in my personal prayer and study life with God, but now I was starting to feel like a failure in disciplines I didn't even know existed!

What Is Church?

After a particularly busy holiday season, I spent the first few days of the New Year cramming for our exam. When test day arrived I scanned the questions to see which ones would cause me problems and did not get past the first one. It read something like, "Did you complete the assignment to pray and journal at least once a week for the duration of this class?—15 points."

To my horror, I realized that I had completely forgotten my professor's warning the first day of class. He had recommended we work on this simple discipline and he would *keep us accountable*. Of course, I couldn't lie about something like that, so I started the test with a minus-15 point handicap. That night, while lying on our family room couch, I had a serious, honest conversation with God for the first time in many years of being a Christian. I asked, "What is my problem? I've known you for twenty years and I can't even spare a few minutes a week to spend time with you. I'm doing all this work for you, preparing to be a minister, and I feel like I don't even know you. All I feel is guilt for not measuring up to the so-called 'standards for Christian leaders.' If this is real life, I don't want any part of it. If you can't show me how to have a real relationship with you, I'm going to stop trying."

Don Williams, a Vineyard pastor and theologian, in his book *Jesus and Addiction*, makes this incredible statement:

> My thesis is simple: We live in an addictive culture that has helped to create a Church made up of addicted and codependent people. If we continue in our denial over this, like drug addicts we shall surely die. If we can break through this denial, then Jesus will set us free, and the Church will live again.[2]

The realization hit me as I sat on the couch that my addictions were out of control. Intervention was required, but it would not take the form of a twelve-step group. I needed a deliverance that could only be initiated by the Spirit of God within my current experience, a personal exodus if you will. That night, God gave me a simple word of direction—Go run a marathon.

The Training Begins

I hate running. In high school, I quit the baseball team because there was too much running and took up golf. That is not exactly the whole truth, of course (I was a terrible hitter and got tired of our coach who yelled all the time). My aversion to running was not because I disliked exercise, although there is considerably less aerobic exertion in golf than pretty much any sport. Runners talk about the *runner's high* and the sensation of moving to the rhythm of their feet pounding on the pavement. As a baseball player, running usually meant you had done some bonehead thing and you were being sent off for a sweaty punishment. The only high I ever got out of running was rounding third and heading to home. Go run a marathon? Insanity.

I searched online and found a few training programs for marathons. They all recommended that anyone attempting to train for a marathon be a regular runner for at least six months. The most I had run recently had been the twenty or so steps from the office to the car door in a rainstorm. I bought some shoes and began to hit the roads around my neighborhood. At first, I could barely muster a mile before I felt like collapsing in a heap. But after a few weeks I was running three or four miles comfortably a few times a week.

By the time I started the actual training, I felt more in shape than I had ever felt in my life. But that did not diminish the fact that I still did not like to run. Every other night, I threw on my running shorts, struggled into my shoes, and took off into the darkness with my headphones. Occasionally, I would have stretches of time when the pace became enjoyable, but it was mostly an act of sheer willpower to keep putting one foot in front of the other. Finally, a year later, we drove to Orlando for the big day. It was in January and happened to be an unusually cold Florida morning. Five and a half hours later, I crossed the finish line among a smattering of people, some twice my age and weight. I still have the Mickey Mouse medal to prove it.

Looking back on that year of training, I better understand what God was trying to accomplish. He was not anticipating that I would fall in love with running or get me to exercise more. I believe God's intention was to distract me. During that year, I began to discover that there was more to knowing God than having a good *quiet time* every morning before work. Maybe God could be found during a run in the sweltering August heat of Florida. Maybe he was there when I saw my running shoes lying in the garage after a tiring day at work. Maybe he would show up at mile 23 when my legs give out and grandmothers start to pass me. He *was* there and I began to see him turn up in surprising ways.

The Armada

One Saturday morning, I was sitting at our dining room table with a pad of paper trying to pray. Extended sessions of prayer have never been my strong suit, so my eyes began wandering around my backyard looking at our wonderful little collection of trees. I was looking at a tall pine tree when God began to bring some thoughts into my mind. I began to see myself as that tree—my new friendship with him was growing the tree straight and quickly stretching upward. Then, I remembered something I'd heard about pine trees on public television—shipbuilders used them for masts because of their height and strength. In my mind, I saw a picture of an old Spanish Galleon, a sailing ship of war. The ship was the community of faith God had in our future, and there were many masts and many sails. Then, a remarkable thing happened: the image zoomed out and I saw countless ships arranged in a battle formation. The word that came to mind was *Armada*. Where was God going with all this?

That day and for the next few weeks I began considering what the church God had in our future might look like. What if church looked less like independent battleships and more like an Armada? Instead of trying to encompass everything under one roof, why not join forces? Maybe churches could be small units of kingdom people who gather together to celebrate their faith in small ways, but then go about the work of subverting the kingdom of darkness in real life. I began to consider the possibility that the American obsession with *bigger is better* had duped us into believing church must be big to be successful. Well, what is success in the kingdom of God? Is it building a monument to my ministry that one day will be torn down to build other monuments? Or does success have more to do with faithfulness, obedience, and love?

Other questions began to haunt my thoughts. Why do churches expend so many resources to host hundreds of people for a worship service once a week? As a church leader, why was I struggling to find the time to meet my neighbors when we supposedly cared so much about *The Lost*? When I talked to people in church about the things I was learning about spiritual disciplines, why did they look at me like I was from Mars? I began to fill notebooks with questions, thoughts, quotes, prayers, and attempted to make sense of what to do next. I knew that whatever was next would not come quickly. I would need time, room to make mistakes, freedom to ask more questions, allies and people to partner with, mothers and fathers, and a heap of patience. However, more than anything else as the journey progressed, I needed some rest.

Into Obscurity

In June of 2001, we moved to West Palm Beach, Florida, as church planters with the Vineyard. My wife, Amber, was six months pregnant with our first child, Jackson. Our original plan was to wait until Jackson was born to move, but in May of that year we lost over three-quarters of our monthly income for the summer. So after much prayer and wrestling with God, we made the decision to sell our house and pull up our roots in Gainesville over a three-week period. We moved with no promise of income and only a short-term living arrangement with Amber's parents. However, we knew we needed to rest. So for three months we did little but eat, sleep in, and engage in our respective favorite pastimes: watching home and garden television and playing golf.

During this time we became acquainted with two ancient and overlooked disciplines: solitude and silence. Knowing only a handful of people in West Palm Beach resulted in most of our time being spent alone or with each other. These long stretches of time and empty space allowed the Spirit to begin his hidden work of interdiction. Remarkably, we found we could get along just fine without the usual patterns of church life that we had grown so accustomed to. We enjoyed leisurely Sunday mornings eating breakfast with Amber's parents. We casually perused books and meditated on Scripture, often just simply reading through Peterson's *The Message*. We occasionally gathered with my brother and sister-in-law, Mark and Alison, and our good friends, Kim and T Freeman. Over dinner, the conversation often led to how God's Spirit was working in our lives. Mark and Ali had been living in West Palm for awhile and were beginning to pull away from a church in which they had faithfully served. Kim and T had moved from Gainesville a year earlier and were rediscovering life in their hometown as a married couple. As *recovering evangelicals*, the six of us were about to enter the wilderness.

What we know about Jesus' forty days in the wilderness is minimal, restricted to a dialogue with Satan after the final day of his fast. We know even less about the approximately thirty years of his life before that day. Jesus' childhood and his work as a carpenter remains somewhat of an enigma; fodder for the creative license of countless authors and filmmakers. Frankly, I'm glad the authors of the gospels left out the details of those unexciting years. Nothing of consequence was built externally other than the products of wood, simple tools, and hard labor. However, I imagine that whatever was accomplished during those thirty years was not only foundational to the last three, but enabled him to say something like this:

> These words I speak to you are not incidental
> additions to your life, homeowner improvements
> to your standard of living. They are foundational
> words, words to build a life on. If you work these
> words into your life, you are like a smart carpenter
> who built his house on solid rock. Rain poured
> down, the river flooded, a tornado hit—but
> nothing moved that house. It was fixed to the rock.
> (Matthew 7.24—25, *The Message*)

What Is Church?

Surely time in obscurity and in the wilderness must have a purpose in the kingdom economy. Even during Jesus' ministry years, he was constantly drawing away from the crowds and pushing away magnified attention. What does it say about the state of the Western church when the accepted practice in church planting is to push through numerical barriers by any means necessary? Why are so many Christian workers broken in exhaustion and either consumed with pride and success or insecurity and failure? Why do deep patterns of sin go left untouched in so-called *Bible-believing* churches? Perhaps Jesus' prophecy has come to fulfillment before our eyes:

> But if you just use my words in Bible studies and don't work them into your life, you are like a stupid carpenter who built his house on the sandy beach. When a storm rolled in and the waves came up, it collapsed like a house of cards.
> (Matthew 7.26–27, *The Message*)

This should strike fear in the heart of anyone who might consider becoming a follower of Jesus. How much more someone embarking on a path towards Christian leadership?

We had once been the shining stars of a growing suburban church, the first to come up through the ranks and become churchplanters. We had all the tools that almost guaranteed our success. The area we were moving to had no Vineyard church in a thirty-mile radius and not much like the Vineyard in worship style. "Just set up shop in a little storefront somewhere," the Voice of Reason said. "Put together a worship band, start a coffee-house, place an ad in the paper, and presto—instant Vineyard. Just take a short rest and then kick it into high gear. You could have a really cool church."

What Is Church?

I believe I would rather have thirty lifetimes of obscurity than ten minutes as pastor of a *cool church*. Obscurity has become a welcome acquaintance, someone who reminds me of my place in the kingdom. A friend of mine has a t-shirt with *I am not famous* written across the chest. To me, anonymity is an incredible gift of the kingdom. No pretense, no show, no masks. Over the first months in West Palm Beach, our world shrank and so did our egos. There would be no replacing of the hamster wheel of church-related activity. We would simply learn how to live—how to *be*—in a new culture with new lives and new relationships.

I often tell people who are considering church planting to take a one-year sabbatical from their common church activities—to detox from church. Purposefully allow their visions and plans to lie fallow for at least a year and simply become a *normal* person. For some, this will be the only means to begin breaking the destructive addictions we have to power, control, and what we think of as godly responsibility. The pastoral call has become an idol that drives an endless cycle of meetings and programs for everything under the sun. Once removed from these idolatrous patterns, the leader is left with the person they have become, for good or ill. Facing the reality of whom we really are—addicted, broken people—is the first step to imagining new life in the kingdom of God.

A Community Forms

In the beginning God created the heavens and the earth. Now the earth was formless and empty, darkness was over the surface of the deep, and the Spirit of God was hovering over the waters. (Genesis 1.1—2).

What Is Church?

Over the past few years, these familiar verses have become a regular meditation. I have imagined our lives and the life of our community in the space between nothing and creation, imagination and concrete reality. In that space there is darkness, but pregnant darkness. It is like waking before the sunrise but knowing that within moments your room will slowly fill with light. Modernity has almost destroyed the joy of that moment, every stitch of time being filled with efficient production and motion. However, forming worlds and human beings is art, and the artist relishes the blank canvas. The energy of this moment cannot be described or comprehended. In the midst of the darkness, there is only the presence of the Spirit, brooding over what he is about to unleash.

There was nothing dramatic about our formation as a community of faith. I usually time the moment of birth around the birthday of our firstborn, Jackson. His entrance into the world signaled that our personal time of rest was over and our corporate life together was beginning. Amidst dirty diapers and restless nights, we began wrestling with how to proceed. How would we approach church with a new foundation? How would this gospel of the kingdom affect us corporately and individually? We quickly identified two corporate disciplines that would be our early guides: silence and asking questions.

Purpose-Driven Deconstruction

Well we know where we're goin'
But we don't know where we've been
And we know what we're knowin'
But we can't say what we've seen
And we're not little children

What Is Church?

And we know what we want
And the future is certain
Give us time to work it out[3]

Why would anyone knowingly subject some of his
or her most basic assumptions about life and faith to a
scrutiny whose outcome is not assured? Is it even possible
to deconstruct with purpose? Can evangelical Christians
in the twenty-first century lay their most preciously held
beliefs on the altar of sacrifice like Abraham did with Issac,
not knowing if they would come away unscathed? I believe
that it is not only possible to deconstruct with purpose, but
essential to the future of the church. The deconstruction
we are most familiar with being done in academic, political,
social, and artistic circles is highly erratic. The violence and
emotion wrapped up in tearing down modern assumptions
can seem justified and even necessary in these contexts,
but will it do in the community of faith?

I have neither the space nor the qualifications to make an
adequate case for the necessity of a period of deconstruction
in current expressions of western Christianity. Regardless
of what debate would arise from such an argument, the
fact remains that the *wheels are coming off* for many people
in North American Christendom. The statistical evidence
from researchers tell a story of a people in search of answers
who are increasingly leaving established churches. The vast
internet community, out of which this book was conceived,
confirms that numerous people across the ecclesiological
landscape are on a quest to discover richer, more dynamic
expressions of faith and community. The question to me is
not if deconstructing modern assumptions about Christian
life *should* occur, but *how?*

I believe we find a model, as with so many other
experiences, for deconstructing assumptions in the life of

Jesus and his immediate followers. Jesus' announcement of the kingdom of God was a ticking time bomb to first century Jewish ears. Was this man the promised Messiah who would deliver the Jews from Roman oppression? Would he bring about the promised return from exile that most Hebrews still believed they were undergoing even after they had returned to their homeland some 400 years before? Would the Israel of old, the Davidic kingdom, a reign of peace, power, and prosperity be ushered in by this simple man from Galilee? Jesus' answer was "Yes, but not in the way that you think."[4] Thus, began during his ministry a three-year journey of unpacking and repacking all those ancient Jewish ideas about Messianic hopes, the kingdom of God, and the true vocation of God's people with a radically new image.

Understand that for our purposes it is just as important *how* Jesus taught his disciples as *what* he taught them. For Jesus, a regular pattern of teaching was to perform a kingdom action and then follow it with a kingdom message. Most recorded healings or miracles performed by Jesus are intertwined by the proclamation of good news, teaching directed at his disciples, or a rebuke aimed at the Jewish religious leaders confronting their most precious assumptions. Deed and word, word and deed: inseparable in the ministry of Jesus. In relationship to his disciples, his retraining of their expectations was anything but erratic. Jesus consistently put his disciples to the test in real life situations, risking his reputation and their trust. These tests came in all shapes and sizes, but their aim was to gradually reveal whom he was and why he had come. Eventually, with the Spirit's guidance, Peter bursts out with the first fruits of Jesus' labor in Matthew 16.16, "You are the Christ, the Son of the living God." The full crop of this retraining would not be reaped until after Jesus' resurrection. As the curtain rises on the book of Acts, a renewed people of God begin the salt and light work Jesus initiated during his ministry.

What Is Church?

Likewise, the deconstruction that we are undergoing in twenty-first century North American Christianity requires both intentionality and risk. We are putting our reputations on the line and risk losing the trust of many desperate people trying to follow Jesus. If that doesn't bring about a measure of holy fear, then maybe we should hesitate before encouraging people to ask a question like, "What is church?" I wonder if it would be appropriate to fully warn someone who wishes to join a community of people engaged in deconstruction that they are getting into dangerous stuff. This is no casual, potluck supper small talk or material for your next Sunday school program. This will probably involve pain not unlike what you experience in grieving the loss of a loved one. There will be frustration, misunderstanding, anger, and hurt feelings. There will be leanings toward a judgmental attitude, the need to release and forgive people or organizations that have caused pain, and the potential for difficult confrontations with friends and family members who are invested in very different paradigms. At all points along the road, there will be the possibility for *total loss*. Some will leave the community of faith altogether. Others will return to a more familiar setting and try to ignore the obvious. But many will remain engaged in the process and stick with each other long enough to reap the harvest of revitalized hope, restored community, and renewed faith.

Have you ever considered that fasting from church could be a spiritual discipline? Now I am not talking about removing yourself from Christian community permanently, but an intentional time of lying fallow for the purposes of recovering your life. That may seem like an oxymoron to some. How can you find life *outside* of church? Nonetheless, Christians are having this experience in growing numbers and simply enjoying their faith together.

Our first eighteen months as a faith community was

in many ways like one prolonged fast from church. This period of time was instrumental in providing a healthy environment for purposeful deconstruction. Let me give a point of clarification here, one that cannot be passed over lightly. Our culture's definition of church is primarily focused on going to a building on Sunday mornings to sing some songs and hear a preacher. Even among the churches that are doing much, much more, the fact remains that the general emphasis is on getting people in the doors on Sunday mornings. That is one reason why I have chosen to use the language *faith community* to describe involvement in a specific, geographic grouping of Christians. *Church* is one of those words that needs quite a lot of unpacking before it can be used indiscriminately.

Our fast really had more to do with removing ourselves from patterns that had become almost mindless. For many of us, the drain of the week-in-week-out cycle of meetings, programs, and events, and the never-ending battle to engage relationally with people in the world had taken its toll. We were in many ways looking for a Sabbath that never seemed to come. Practically, this meant that we had to take intentional steps towards being *unbusy*. As Dallas Willard has said, *unbusyness* does not mean lack of action. It simply means that we would do things deliberately slow, giving our actions time to catch up with our thoughts.

The first natural step for us was laying down any aspirations of experiencing rapid numerical growth. This community simply would not grow quickly. Period. As I write this now, it seems to be such a simple, agreeable thing to say. However, I fully realize that the demon of bigness will not die quickly. So how did we as evangelicals reconcile our seemingly innate desire to minister on a colossal scale? Well, it began with coming to grips with our incredible shortsightedness. Has the church *always* existed as an organization primarily centered on numerical growth? Has the Holy Spirit *only* given his attention and blessing to the evangelistic calling of the church? Have authentic expressions of discipleship to Jesus *only* come in communities that invest most of their time and energy recruiting new members?

Richard Foster, in his book *Streams of Living Water* writes:

> Today a mighty river of the Spirit is bursting forth from the hearts of women and men, boys and girls. It is a deep river of divine intimacy, a powerful river of holy living, a dancing river of jubilation in the Spirit, and a broad river of unconditional love for all peoples. As Jesus says, "Out of the believer's heart shall flow rivers of living water." (John 7.38)

The astonishing new reality in this mighty flow of the Spirit is how sovereignly God is bringing together streams of life that have been isolated from one another for a very long time. This isolation is completely understandable from a historical perspective. Over the centuries some precious teaching or vital experience is neglected until, at the appropriate moment, a person or movement arises to correct the omission. Numbers of people come under the renewed teaching, but soon vested interests and a host of other factors come into play, producing resistance to the renewal, and the new movement is denounced. In time it forms its own structures and community life, often in isolation from other Christian communities.

This phenomenon has been repeated many times through the centuries. The result is that various

streams of life—good streams, important streams—
have been cut off from the rest of the Christian
community, depriving us all of a balanced vision of
life and faith.[5]

As a community, we needed an extensive baptism in all
these *streams*.[6] However, this seems simpler than it really is.
How do you go about learning 2000 years of church history
and practice without being utterly overwhelmed? Take
prayer, for example. The history and experience of Christian
prayer is so immense that one group of people could easily
spend a generation simply studying and practicing to
become informed pray-ers. Gratefully, the kingdom of God
makes room for all levels of experience. There is no caste
system in Christian discipline. In a very real way, we are all
beginners, all infants in a world far larger than what we can
see, smell, touch, taste, and hear.

So like toddlers we must give ourselves space to have
free play in God's kingdom. As a faith community, we
experimented with forms of prayer that were very foreign
to our experience. We substituted the sofa or dinner table
for a pulpit. We stayed up until the wee hours on Saturday
night and slept in on Sundays. We threw parties and hung
out at the beach. If there was one sin we could accurately
be accused of, it would be gluttony. This would be obvious
if you looked at our group expenditures for the first year. In
short, we replaced the busyness of common church activity
with simple practices, ancient and contemporary, that can
be enjoyed with little preparation. Our times together
became very simple and increasingly informal. *Where two or
three are gathered in my name* became a living reality instead
of a platitude expressed during a formal gathering. Our
fast succeeded in pushing us farther and farther away from
relying on planned meetings and toward a fluid, integrated
community of disciples. As a church planter, this process of

detoxing from church was having a profound impact on my self-identification as a pastor and leader. Redefining my own role would become a critical next step as we dove deeper into the questions we were asking and life as disciples of Jesus we were attempting to live.

Chapter Three
The Death of a Pastor

P*astor* is such a pleasant sounding word. It conjures a sensation that no matter what insanity is going on, there are people around who will not be easily rattled, who will pray for you, sit with you while you weep, counsel you when you are confused, be there for the celebrations and for the grief.

I have a history with the word pastor because I was trained to be one, at least in the classic sense. From an evangelical perspective, the image that the word *pastor* invokes is fairly defined on surface issues yet carries with it a multitude of variations in its deeper practice. Depending on your heritage, *pastor* might take on that dignified, elegant tone and bring to mind images of a gentle man presiding over a community's spiritual needs. It could also mean one who is an impassioned orator who weekly storms the stage pleading with the congregation to hear and live the word of God. *Pastor* might look like a business executive, carrying out managerial responsibilities in the context of a frenetic, entrepreneurial enterprise. Or it could be the one the community looks to in times of crisis as a rock of stability and faith, having all the right words and prayers to say for any occasion.

There are other images, of course, but the one thread that runs through them all is the singularity of one man or woman fulfilling the vision of what it means to be pastor in their specific context. What if, for the sake of argument, all of those visions of what a pastor is or does could be set aside? What if a pastor is not a person who leads the church, preaches, holds office hours for counseling, heads the elder board, visits people in the hospital, officiates at weddings, and puts on a nice face to people in the community? Those activities may have pastoral elements, and certainly a pastoral gifting would help in order to carry them out, but a pastor they do not make. Instead, what if the word *pastor* could be put on the shelf for awhile? Not thrown in the trash or dragged through the dirt, but simply retired for a season. What would that do to the way we think about how church works? How would that affect our understanding of Christian leadership? Or organizational structure? Preaching? Caregiving? Ministry?

Not too long after our church formed, I began to have a serious identity crisis. At the time, I was helping Amber teach music to preschoolers in order for us to provide for our little family. The group was giving us a small monthly stipend, yet I was beginning to wonder why. Most of our energy as a church was directed towards learning how to be disciples of Jesus in our real lives, not just during church events. Consequently, there was little for a traditional pastor-type person to, well, *do*. We met for worship in a home, so there was no overhead or infrastructure to maintain. Most of our group times were heavily oriented towards discussion and practicing spiritual disciplines together, so there was not much preparation necessary. If someone needed counsel, no one expected me to be the one always available. After all, I did have a job and, besides, we were asking so many questions that no one believed that one person could actually have all the answers anyway. Eventually, the stark realization hit me squarely between the eyes—being a pastor to these people mostly meant that I just *be a disciple and do what disciples do*. That was a relief on one hand, and terrifying on the other. I could relax a little from what I was discovering were expectations that no one was placing on me other than myself. However, I had not been trained to just be a disciple alongside other disciples. I had been trained to *run a church*.

Eugene Peterson tells a story that illustrates the world in which most pastors have been formed:

> I was traveling with a pastor I respected very much. I was full of zest and vision, anticipating pastoral life. My inner conviction of call to the pastorate was about to be confirmed by others. What God wanted me to do, what I wanted to do, and what others wanted me to do were about to converge.
>
> From fairly extensive reading about pastor and priest predecessors, I was impressed that everyday pastoral life was primarily concerned with developing a life of prayer among the people. Leading worship, preaching the gospel, and teaching Scripture on Sundays would develop in the next six days into representing the life of Christ in the human traffic of the everyday.

What Is Church?

With my mind full of these thoughts, my pastor friend and I stopped at a service station for gasoline. My friend, a gregarious person, bantered with the attendant. Something in the exchange provoked a question.

What do you do?

I run a church.

No answer could have surprised me more. I knew, of course, that pastoral life included institutional responsibilities, but it never occurred to me that I would be defined by those responsibilities. But the moment I became ordained, I found I was so defined both by the pastors and executives over me and by the parishioners around me. The first job description given me omitted prayer entirely.[1]

As a church planter, I was trained to create a viable, sustainable organization as fast as possible. How I did it was not the important thing, only that I reached certain numerical benchmarks quickly enough to show that the church could be considered a *real church*. To prepare me for this task, I needed to develop a fairly complex skill set: theological expertise, leadership qualities, counseling tools, conflict resolution, business principles, event coordination, effective advertising, and familiarization with popular culture just to name a few. In order to be successful, I needed to handpick a team of qualified individuals (all volunteer, of course) to be committed to the grueling process of launching the church. Those team members must be completely clear on what my vision for the church was and how it would be carried out. During the period of the actual process of starting the church, I was to anticipate being under extreme stress both personally and in my family life. Due to the fact that financial support within my denomination was limited, it was inferred that I would need to hold a second job in order to pay the bills. The intention, of course, was to rapidly build an organization that could support at least my own full-time salary through offerings. Realistically, that meant we needed to have around 100 people attending Sunday services in order for that to be viable.

Giving the modern church planter a title like *pastor* seems a tad inappropriate when faced with these realities. Church planting, across denominational lines and the theological spectrum, is fundamentally spiritual entrepreneurship. There is not much different about planting a church than opening a good restaurant or a real estate office. It requires the same time commitment, training, sacrifice, financial investment and risk. One obvious difference is that most of your labor force will be volunteer, but everything that is true about the consumer in America will be true for you. Any church that does not guilt its congregation into sticking around will be left with the task of creating an environment where people will choose to stay, because it *will* be a choice. As an entrepreneur, the church planter must be able to create a satisfying corporate culture from the beginning if he or she has any chance of survival.

You might be wondering at this point why I am describing this process in such a clinical manner. What about God's intervention in all this? Isn't this why church planters pray? In the end, isn't it up to God to bring people into his church? In the 1990s, Todd Hunter completed a study on why church plants fail. He collected data from churches all over the country that had folded for various reasons or never quite reached a sustainable level of attendees. What he found generally was that the failing churches lacked a leader with a clear sense of call. They may or may not have had vision for a particular kind of church, but vision was not as critical as *calling* when it came to survival. Pastoring in twenty-first century America is an undertaking for the stout of heart. Spiritual entrepreneurship requires a certain amount of callousness towards the process. You will be disappointed. Success will seem totally out of your control and failure entirely your fault. In the end, the majority will give the outcome completely to God and simply do what they know how to do best. However, what cannot be ignored is that church planting and much of what is considered *pastoral work*, at least for the past few decades in America, is unequivocally more like running a business than anything else.

Take the Best and Go

Early in my transition, I struggled often with feeling ashamed for the thoughts I was having. If I did not follow the expected pattern of church planting, would I simply be wimping out? Was I just lazy? Unable to handle the stress and work load? Could I really pursue the calling I felt God had placed on my life without planting a church in the way I had been trained?

The founder of the Vineyard, John Wimber, died in 1997. Although I appreciated what Wimber had done during his life and ministry, my connection to the Vineyard was not directly from him like so many others in the movement. I was saddened by his early passing, but his prophetic admonition to the Vineyard before he died rang in my ears: *Take the best and go.* Wimber expected the next generation to continue teaching people about the kingdom of God, praying for the sick, casting out demons, bringing the Good News to the world. But as a young almost-church-planter, what did *Take the best and go* really mean?

What Is Church?

With my imagination stretched, I attended the 1999 Vineyard National Pastor's Conference in Anaheim, California. Towards the end of the conference, Todd Hunter addressed the crowd. As he began, ushers passed out a thick set of notes he had prepared with the title "The Church I Would Build." I heard a few groans and chuckles from some of the people around me (pastors are a notoriously difficult bunch when you get more than a handful of them in the same room). But as Todd began to speak, I was enthralled with his message. Here was someone who had done his homework and appreciated the enormity of the questions we faced as a movement and as the church at large. As he continued, tears began to roll down my face. This man who I barely knew and had only met once or twice was asking some of the same questions I was asking. Afterwards, Amber and I approached Todd and ask him to pray for us. He politely did and we had a brief conversation. Todd gave us some friendly advice and we parted ways, however, the damage was done. Present in the auditorium that day and in the next years to come were young men and women who were in desperate need of advocates, *champions*, who could help us navigate the storm of transition.

I took Todd's notes home from that conference and studied them. I began to research the books he recommended and learn the language. One of the phrases that he used captured my imagination and still does to this day—missional communities. What if we began to think of church as something other than an organization where religious goods and services change hands? Missional communities were groups of people who did not exist to find more warm bodies to fill up pews or pay the pastor's salary. They looked outward, to represent the kingdom of God for the sake of the world. However, simultaneously they were a *community*, a family. They did life together and discovered God's unique call, individually and corporately, to be a blessing to the world around them. Maybe this is what Wimber meant by *Take the best and go?* Take the best... and *go out.* Obviously, there would be a need for distinctive leadership, something quite unlike the dominant models for leadership existing in the church at the time.

Between-the-Times Leadership

One day I was at a friend's house for dinner and happened to glance at his bookshelf. One title caught my eye: *Missional Church: A Vision for the Sending of the Church in North America.* I asked to borrow it and immediately began reading later that evening. What I discovered was that the rabbit trail I was chasing went farther and was better traveled than I had thought. Here were six scholars, university professors as well as church leaders, who were verbalizing many of the same questions and calling to account the leadership practices I was now beginning to reconsider. In Chapter Seven, Alan Roxburgh states the problem with aplomb,

> Moreover, across the varieties of today's models of ministry, there remains this underlying notion of church leadership functioning as specialized professionals. Whether the leadership is that of the social activist, the megachurch entrepreneur, or the therapist-pastor, all are seen to require some aspect of professionalized training.

> This view effectively eclipses the gifts for leadership in the non-ordained contingent of God's sent people, those known in Christendom as the laity. Ministry remains identified with the static roles of clergy as priest, pedagogue, or professional, all dispensers of

spiritual resources. Even where the priesthood of all
believers stands as a theological conviction...it is rarely
practiced in the church.[2]

Despite the best efforts of modern church leadership,
the average churchgoer is unable to fully and freely express his
or her leadership gifts. As one who was training for *professional
ministry*, this was a sobering realization. The well–known
Pareto principle, twenty percent of the resources perform
eighty percent of the work, seems to be more of an excuse
for church leaders than a driver towards improving that ratio.
Most efforts to improve things simply create more activity,
but are not releasing people into their God-given callings. In
order for the kingdom of God to become a reality for the *whole
church*, a comprehensive transition is required. Roxburgh calls
the people who are leading this transition, *between-the-times
leaders*:

> They are re-forming a collection of consumer, needs-
> centered individuals to live by an alternative narrative.
> Making a transition from the optimism of modernity to
> the humility of a people in exile evokes the experience of
> brokenness. Voicing this brokenness enables churches to
> feel the gulf between their present forms and covenant
> community of Jesus.[3]

The modern church leader does not have time for
brokenness. There are too many lost people out there, too many
programs to manage, too many spiritual problems to solve with
spiritual technology. Yet the fact remains, the organizational
efforts of the American church have not produced disciples
of Jesus. The well-documented mass departure from these
organizations is evidence of the brokenness that exists, yet
remains unacknowledged. Helping people verbalize what they
see and feel, to learn to ask good questions, becomes one of
the first tasks of the between-the-times leader:

Evoking this voice is a deeply pastoral task. Leadership evokes, opens, and brings forth the experience of confusion and brokenness waiting to be given expression in the church today. A people who have grasped their brokenness understand that the reign of God is received as a gift. It is at this point that one can appropriate the covenant nature of the missional community.[4]

Years after first reading *Missional Church*, I discovered that Chapter Seven had a similar impact on many of the new friends I was meeting who were engaging in this kind of transitional leadership. We were

The death of a Pastor...the death of a title...

individually coming to conclusions that were eerily similar, yet would be worked out uniquely in the small groups of people we were gathering with in our hometowns. One of these conclusions was that it was increasingly difficult to call ourselves pastors, although as Roxburgh states, what we were doing was fundamentally a pastoral work. The death of a Pastor was really the death of a title, a place in the good ol' boys club of professional ministry. It was also the death of pastoral leadership as maintenance of a religious organization.

The death I experienced as a pastor did not come easily or painlessly, and I was by no means alone in my suffering. I struggled for months trying to imagine my role in this little community of friends who were meeting in a house in Palm Beach Gardens. Through a series of events, I began working as an engineer again at my father-in-law's consulting firm. This took some of the immediacy of the question off my mind, yet I still could not conceive how I could be of any use to a group of people wrestling with this daunting transition. I needed a new definition, a new understanding of who I was that made sense of where we were going.

What Is Church?

Pastor: Spiritual Orienteer

Orienteering is a sport that I have never tried but has always piqued my curiosity. It is a simple sport, but holds the unique synthesis of physical stamina and mental acuity under pressure in order to complete an overland course in the shortest time possible. The closest I have ever come to participating in something like orienteering would be the scavenger hunts we used to have in college in Campus Crusade. Our campus director would provide clues pointing us to obscure locations all over Gainesville. Invariably, we would run from one location to the next, sweating, panting, and trying to make sense of some crazy riddle. Although stressful at times, the joy of the scavenger hunt was watching the unique talents emerge from the group along the way. One person would hunker down as the riddle solver focusing all their mental energy and producing answers to guide us to the next location. Another would have a knack for navigation on the crowded Gainesville highways. Someone else would race from the car to the place where the clue was hidden and back before any other teams could get theirs. The best teams were the ones who could manage the frantic pace yet keep a calm enough demeanor to not drive fifty miles out of the way because of a wrongly interpreted clue.

Trying to be a disciple of Jesus is confusing, exhausting, and downright frustrating at times. But as with orienteering or scavenger hunts, learning how the riddles fit together and the compass points us along the path to the next point of discovery can be an exhilarating experience. A good definition of *spirituality* is the comprehensive and concrete practice of living life with the awareness of the presence and interaction of Someone or Something who is involved with us and our world. In Christian spirituality, that Someone is God the Father through Jesus by the Spirit and He is intimately invested in a preferred outcome for our life—living as his disciples as agents of his kingdom. We are to be changed, transformed, to become like him, to be able to naturally and freely love and do good. However, the path to entering this kind of life is not without tremendous struggle and travail. Sometimes the riddles just don't make any sense. We lose our compass in the mud. We get blisters and ankle sprains. We get into fights with our teammates. It rains. The other teams hide the clues to the next location (which happened on more than one occasion in our scavenger hunts). And most often, we just give up because working through the course is just too damn hard.

This is why pastoral leadership in its current forms is inadequate. We were never meant to go along for the ride while someone else solves the riddles, checks the compass and the map, and then marks out a path to the next checkpoint. Pretty soon even the most rugged and experienced guide will get discouraged. However, the greater chance is that they will from time to time (and even frequently in some cases) just be dead wrong. Fifty miles later and not a clue in sight, you begin to wonder why you're playing the game in the first place. Spiritual orienteers recognize that they are people who are learning how to play the game in harmony with other orienteers and with the Spirit. These are not guides who see themselves as the only person who will get the team from point A to point B. Nor do they reduce the game to an individual effort that destroys the free-flowing leadership the Spirit provides to gently nudge (or forcefully push) the team to each goal.

So what might this role look like in practice? Spiritual orienteers are not content to plod along with the status quo, performing the expected functions of church leadership. They dive into the depths of God's riches in prayer, in the

Scriptures, in His mind and His thoughts. Together they search for answers to the growing-edge questions posed by the community. They pursue the wisdom of other saints and guides that have gone before and completed the course. Some are gifted in understanding about how God works and what He cares about. Others point out new pathways the Spirit opens to deeper maturity and fruit. And some simply pick up the wounded and carry them to safety. Orienteers do not need a title or a salary to do their job. Some may be resourced by the community for a time for a particular purpose. However, the true orienteer is in the game for the pure joy of getting to the next level and helping others do the same. He or she has the same mindset Paul had in his Ephesians 4 vision for the church:

> ...to prepare God's people for works of service, so that the body of Christ may be built up until we all reach unity in the faith and in the knowledge of the Son of God *and become mature, attaining to the whole measure of the fullness of Christ.* (Ephesians 4.12–13)

This is true pastoring. The central focus of leadership is Jesus himself. We get to be in his game and play according to his rules, which really are not rules at all but a flowing stream of love, wisdom, and power that we collectively tap into. The spiritual orienteers are the ones not afraid to get dirty. They often get tired, which is why there must be plenty of them to go around, but their value to the community's health and fruitfulness is essential and irreplaceable. This was a vision of leadership I could become comfortable with in spite of the discomfort of transition. The net effect for those other orienteers around me was the understanding that this church was not Mike's baby. My identity was focused on being a disciple, a good husband

and father, and someone who demonstrated to others the way forward in a dark and confusing land.

Leading from Behind

Recently *Rev.* magazine conducted an interview with John Maxwell with the title, "If I Had It to Do Over Again." Maxwell, of course, is an author, speaker, and *leadership guru* to countless pastors and business leaders. In the interview, Maxwell was asked to look back at thirty-plus years of pastoral ministry and leadership training:

> Rev!: What would you do differently if you were starting over today?
>
> Maxwell: I'd have a lot less church; I'd have less programs; I'd have less services. I'd have a lot less of everything.
>
> Rev!: Why?
>
> Maxwell: As a pastor I've made a lot of mistakes, but one of my major mistakes was thinking that life revolved around the local church and what we were doing. For example, if you were a member of the church, you had to have a ministry in the church. That was a huge mistake. I had high-capacity people in my church doing things that were pretty mundane for business people. If I had it to do over again, I'd have people doing a lot more ministry outside the church, in their workplace or in their community or in their volunteer organizations. I'd find out where they had the greatest influence and make their ministry where their greatest influence was, not confine it to a church. Huge mistake I made. And I didn't see it until I was

out, but I was too inward. I had a lot of high-capacity
people who were probably never "salt and light" like
they could have been. I'd change that immediately if
I went back to the local church. I'd be much more into
how we influenced the community and a lot less into
'How can I get everybody onboard with my church
and with my program?'[5]

In 2007, the most famous (and copied) megachurch
in America, Willow Creek Community Church, released
results from a *multi-year qualitative study*[6] they conducted
for self-evaluation. Executive pastor, Greg Hawkins, and
the founding pastor of Willow, Bill Hybels, presented the
study at a leadership summit. Their findings, in essence,
were that participation in a church's ministries or programs
does not predict whether someone will become a deeper
disciple of Jesus. Hawkins put it this way, "Increasing levels
of participation in these sets of activities does NOT predict
whether someone's becoming more of a disciple of Christ.
It does NOT predict whether they love God more or they
love people more."[6]

They determined that the resources and leadership
they had invested in drawing people into these programs
did not produce the results they had hoped for. Hybels
made this blunt confession.

> Some of the stuff that we have put millions of dollars
> into, thinking it would really help our people grow
> and develop spiritually, when the data actually came
> back, it wasn't helping people that much. Other things
> that we didn't put that much money into and didn't
> put much staff against is stuff our people are crying
> out for.[7]

What Is Church?

In the end, Willow Creek determined that people need more focused care in supporting their development as disciples of Jesus. But more importantly, they saw that leadership misses the mark when it does not take into account the uniqueness of people and how they grow. Bill Hybels and John Maxwell, two of the biggest names in evangelical church leadership, were coming to similar conclusions and recognizing they would have done things differently. What does this say about leadership moving forward?

The type of leadership Hybels and Maxwell advocated for years demanded a strong, up-front personality. The vision-caster. The idea man. The prophet. This leader would set direction for the church in a visible manner that could not be missed. But what if the kind of leadership necessary to help people become disciples, to love God and neighbor more, does not primarily happen from the *front*? What if it looks more like leading from *behind*?

The Good Shepherd Redux

Leading from behind sounds like an oxymoron, but perhaps that is because our imaginations towards leadership have been so thoroughly captured by the *leader as hero* imagery. Another reason might be cultural. Maybe outside of North America or Europe there are models for leadership that better approximate this dynamic.

When we think of Jesus as the Good Shepherd, we typically imagine him sitting down in some peaceful, green field, while a flock of perfectly white sheep slowly graze on perfectly green grass. It is not an image of Jesus we Americans identify with well. We are much more like the Romans than we care to admit. We want to see the kick-butt Jesus: turning over tables, going head-to-head with demons, insulting the people in charge of religion. In fact, there are some in our culture who believe that this is the only Jesus worth emulating. The *Good Shepherd* imagery is too quiet, too weak, too pastoral.

We would not consider Nelson Mandela to be too quiet or too weak from a leadership perspective. Credited as being the driving force behind the move to abolish apartheid in South Africa, his leadership has been anything but weak. However, in a recent interview in the Harvard Business Review, Linda Hill describes how a story from Mandela's autobiography portrayed a rather unexpected image of his leadership style:

> Several years ago—jetlagged in my hotel room in Cape Town, overlooking Robben Island, where Mandela had been imprisoned—I was reading his autobiography, *Long Walk to Freedom*. At the time, I was working on an article about leadership in the twenty-first century, and I came across a passage in which Mandela recalls how a leader of his tribe talked about leadership: 'A leader, he said, is like a shepherd. He stays behind the flock, letting the most nimble go out ahead, whereupon the others follow, not realizing that all along they are being directed from behind.'

> To me, this take on the shepherd image embodies the kind of leader we increasingly need: someone who understands how to create a context or culture in which other people are willing and able to lead. This image of the shepherd behind his flock is an acknowledgment that leadership is a collective activity in which different people at different times—depending on their strengths, or 'nimbleness'—come forward to move the group in the direction it needs to go. The metaphor also hints at the agility of a group that doesn't have to

What Is Church?

wait for and then respond to a command from the front. That kind of agility is more likely to be developed by a group when a leader conceives of her role as creating the opportunity for collective leadership, as opposed to merely setting direction.[8]

What Hill and Mandela recognized is that there are some leadership tasks that cannot be accomplished through direct means. A shepherd who expects his sheep to fall in line and follow his every move will not be a shepherd for long. Mandela had to create an environment that made it possible for people to believe in a world without racist divisions. Implicitly, he understood this was impossible to accomplish alone, from a place of power. As a result, Hill began studying how in today's global, rapidly changing economy, business leaders cannot accomplish their goals through brow beating their employees or customers. A new vision of leadership is required, one that is unfamiliar to the get-things-done hero at the front of the pack.

Maybe the *Good Shepherd* is a more radical idea of leadership than we have been led to believe. When Jesus laid down his life for his sheep, he did more than save them—he created the opportunity for them to be released to the world, to go out ahead of the flock and discover new territory. What if Jesus had not died when he did? Would the disciples have ever *gotten it?* Would they have been able to bring the gospel to all nations? There were countless would-be *Messiahs* in the first century whose followers never became anything more than an enclave of self-preservation. When the *Messiah* died, they died. The followers of Jesus were different because Jesus understood that the kind of change God wanted would not come from a place of power. His kingdom would come through God's power being released to his followers. "I tell you the truth, unless a kernel of wheat falls to the ground and dies, it remains

66

only a single seed. But if it dies, it produces many seeds."
(John 12.24)

Early on in the life of our church, I recognized that my leadership would either result in the community experiencing a quick death or the opportunity for a long life. The death would not come from external forces, a lack of organization, vision, or resources. It would come from my ego—my need to *be somebody* in the church leadership culture. In order to make a name for myself, I needed to be a gatherer of leaders and marketer of our church-product. If they bought into my plan fast enough, people would take notice. But what I would gain in recognition, I would lose in possibility. The future would now be up to me. Nothing would be possible unless I made it happen. One day I would be left with a desperate attempt to pass my leadership to another ego, or be faced with the sad reality that the church would simply die right along with me.

The *opportunity for a long life* is really the opportunity for the people of God to reach their full potential. The goal is not to create an organization that stands the test of time. The goal is to continue carrying the gospel to the nations, to make it possible for people to believe in a world where God is in charge. I cannot do this by myself. A church cannot do this as an enclave of self-preservation. The only real possibility is to stubbornly (and perhaps, foolishly) persist in creating a culture where the nimble can go out ahead and lead into new territory. This, of course, all happens in the messy and beautiful context of community.

Chapter Four
The Failure of Community

One afternoon a few years ago I received a phone call at work from a friend in our church. He did not sound well, but he was not sick. We agreed to meet that night for coffee to talk about whatever was troubling him.

On the way to the coffee shop that night, I did not know what had happened but I knew it was serious. During that drive, God spoke some gentle words to me about loving him no matter the cost and that my friend would do what it took to recover. Not knowing what that meant exactly, I sat down at the coffee shop to hear his story. It turned out that his wife had discovered that morning that he had been having an affair. There was nothing unusual about this man or his family. They had both been pastor's kids and had left their previous church on good terms. Sure, they had huge questions like the rest of us, but there was nothing visible that set them apart from the rest of the community. They were *on the journey* with us—in silence, laughter, and tears. But yet, as we would find out later, my friend had been sexually addicted and living a double life for years. As I listened to his story, there was one thought that kept running through my mind: *If the kingdom of God is not available to him, right now in the middle of this mess, then why are we wasting our time?* Somehow that gave me an immense amount of hope, much more hope than I should have had.

As the rest of that week progressed, the cycle of shock, compassion, anger, and acceptance took our entire community for the ride of our lives. Surprisingly I saw the same kind of hope manifested in the different personalities of the group, but it did not come without a cost. We were hopeful for our friend, that he would recover his life and save his family. We were hopeful that this experience would show us the reality and power of the kingdom in the darkest, most hopeless situations. We were hopeful that God would continue to shine his light in the darkest parts of the rest of us. But after our friend's confession, relationships in our community became strained and there was a period of separation and isolation. I became busier at work and we had our second child. Others simply did not spend as much time with each other anymore. Our gatherings were more subdued and sometimes awkward. We were beginning to face the fact that our dream of community had failed, or precisely the failure of the kind of community I had hoped for. Thankfully, I had already found others around the country who were experiencing many of the same challenges.

> We were hopeful that God...

What Is Church?

Finding Each Other, Then Losing Some

In the spring of 2002, I began a website and blog, (www. whatischurch.com). Initially my hope was to create another space for our local community to have conversations and write about our journey. I also hoped to connect with others in the West Palm Beach area who might be thinking about church differently. What I did not expect happened within a few months after we began writing. I began receiving emails from people, a few as far away as New Zealand, who were asking similar questions and enjoying reading our thoughts. Soon, in early 2003, I had the privilege of connecting with other people who had similar influences. In January of that year, many of us traveled to Boise, Idaho, to join with Todd Hunter and Mark Priddy, the founder of Allelon,[1] to talk about what we were learning and how we could support one another. Over the course of the next three years, a core of about twelve couples representing faith communities from all over the U.S. began to deepen our relationship. Most of us held denominational affiliations and we were intent on keeping those ties. This was not the beginning of a movement—we had too many questions for something like that. Mostly what we desired from one another was friendship, encouragement, and *understanding*. We needed to talk to others who understood what we were experiencing, the pain we were enduring, but also the freedom we were beginning to taste.

During the first week of March 2006, we were all preparing to convene at the Brownhouse, one of the community houses of Vineyard Central[2] in Cincinnati. The Brownhouse was the place we had agreed would be our primary gathering place, as there was plenty of housing around and was central for most of the Midwest families. We had grown accustomed to sitting on the back porch, with perhaps a nice dark beer or smooth cigar, and enjoying the kind of conversation and exchange of *life* that had become so important to each of us. This particular weekend was to be an important time together. We were going to discuss candidly where we saw our relationship heading and how we could be more of a blessing and encouragement to each other. Also, one of our friends from Columbus, Mark Palmer, seemed to be losing his battle with cancer and we wanted to again gather to lay hands on him and pray for healing.

On Friday the third, a week before we were to gather, I got a phone call with some disturbing news. Chad Canipe, one of the guys from the Cincinnati area, had gone into the hospital. He had been struggling with what he thought was walking pneumonia, but now was having trouble breathing. Over the weekend, the news got worse. Chad's lungs began hemorrhaging and he was placed on a respirator. As the days passed, his condition seemed to become increasingly confusing to the doctors and critical. By the time I boarded the plane with Amber on Thursday afternoon, Chad was unconscious, unresponsive, and in need of a miracle. Thursday evening, we had a small reunion with some of our friends, but mostly prayed and waited to hear more news about Chad. Friday morning, I rode with Chris Marshall, also from Cincinnati, to pick up Eric Keck who was flying in from Vermont. As we neared the airport, Chris' cell phone rang. It was Kevin Rains, a close friend of Chad's and one of the leaders of Vineyard Central. Kevin broke the news: Chad had passed.

Chris and I continued to ride to the airport in a state of shock. Chris had known Chad for a number of years, and he along with Kevin and Glenn Johnson from Oxford, Ohio, had formed a *Fight Club* of sorts, a regular time to share their questions and revelations, their joy and their pain. As we picked up Eric and broke the news to him, there was really not much we could say. Immediately we drove to the hospital to see Kevin and his wife Tracy who had spent the night there with Chad's family. We spent a few minutes with Chad's parents and cousin, who were obviously still in a daze. Both Chad's father and cousin were pastors, and his entire family had been convinced that he was going to be healed.

Kevin, Chris, Eric, and I then walked into Chad's room to say goodbye. As I am writing this, the image of Chad, an enormously strong and healthy thirty-four year old man lying on that bed, is etched into my mind. We sat silent for a while, praying, wondering, listening. I thought, "That could be me lying there." And then, "Why *shouldn't* that be me lying there?" After a few more minutes, I broke the silence, "Guys, this isn't just about sitting around smoking cigars on the back porch anymore." We were no longer a few casual friends, joined by common questions and similar hopes. We were now at war.

The next day, a few of us traveled to Columbus to spend time with Mark Palmer, his wife Amy, and son Micah, and friends from his faith community, The Landing Place.[3] Mark had been too weak for the two hour drive to Cincinnati, so we decided to take the gathering to him. Half of the group went into Mark's room and spent time praying and talking with him, and the other half including Amber and I sat downstairs with the Landing Place *kids*, as we affectionately call them. They were a tired bunch having given out so much to Mark and Amy during his illness. Questions about what would happen if Mark died had barely been asked or considered. They carried hope, but were desperately in need of companions through whatever they would have to endure next. We ministered as best as we could, although not much was making sense on that day, just over twenty-four hours from losing Chad.

What Is Church?

The morning after Jesus' crucifixion must have been excruciating for the disciples. I can imagine them going through the standard cycle of emotions: shock, confusion, anger, hopelessness, sorrow. The gospel of John records that the disciples had locked themselves in a room for fear of what the Jews might do if they found them. I am sure that some of them even felt foolish for believing that the end for this *Messiah* would turn out any different. Again, their hopes for the kingdom of God had been dashed. Again, they would have to wait for another to come, unless they died first. I don't think disillusionment would be a strong enough word for what they felt. Why had Jesus gathered them, demonstrated so many unbelievable signs and wonders, and trained them in the kingdom way of life only to leave them huddled in a room afraid to go outside for fear of suffering the same fate as their Master?

In the midst of this confusion, not too soon, but not too late, Jesus reappears with a simple message: "Peace be with you. As the Father sent me, so I send you." (John 20.21) His message is clear; their work is not over. The disciples did not immediately leave their locked room and begin evangelizing Israel and beyond as the following paragraphs in John describe the disciples still in their room a week later. Luke writes, "After his suffering he presented himself alive to them by many convincing proofs, appearing to them during forty days and speaking about the kingdom of God. While staying with them, he ordered them not to leave Jerusalem, but to wait there for the promise of the Father." (Acts 1.3–4) Shortly they were infused with the Holy Spirit's power and began their missionary work with stunning results.

As I write this, our group of friends still reside somewhere in those forty days of waiting. Many of us who have experienced an exodus into the good news of God's kingdom are still waiting to see where all of this will lead us. Our friend locally found healing for his sexual addiction and the first fruits of a changed life, but left the community not long after. A few weeks after fervently praying for Mark Palmer's healing that March afternoon, he finally lost his long battle with cancer. I am sure there will be some who will read this book and think, "Is that it? What is so remarkable about what these people are writing about? Where are the results, the salvations, the healings? I want to see the fruit!" Frankly the fruits of our labor have been meager numerically. Most of our churches are only comprised of twenty or so people, some have a few more. But when I look at my friends—in spite of the data to the contrary—I see something I have rarely seen before in my life as a Christian. I see people who have escaped hell. People that could be sitting in the same pew every Sunday morning, week after week. People who could be running churches yet losing their souls. What is unjust is that these people's voices have not been heard by this generation, because the church continues to dismiss their value. They are not successful enough to be heard, at least according to the established metrics. If that is true, then I respectfully propose that we need to reconsider our definition of success.

Becoming Disillusioned

The failure of community is the failure of our strategies for designing a church that fulfills our preconceived notions of what church should be. A few years ago, I saw a website of a new, emerging church that was using the house church model. The information on the site led me to believe there already existed a somewhat developed network of house churches that were utilizing this structure to facilitate their relationship. But when I clicked on the *House Church*

Locator, I found this: "Our church was founded in October 2001 and currently consists of one House Plant in northern ____. Click here to see how we plan to grow." How we *plan to grow?* Why appear to be something you are not? It is easy to become attached to our methods and models; to enamor ourselves with a particular postmodern innovation or how we have *recaptured the essence of early church life.* That is surely a recipe for disaster. Become enamored with Jesus. Fall in love with his people. Choose to serve them first, not a strategy.

The failure of community is also the failure of the dream of community. Dietrich Bonhoeffer, in his famous book on Christian community, *Life Together*, makes these haunting statements:

> Innumerable times a whole Christian community has broken down because it had sprung from a wish dream. The serious Christian, set down for the first time in a Christian community, is likely to bring with him a very definite idea of what Christian life together should be and to try to realize it. But God's grace speedily shatters such dreams. Just as surely as God desires to lead us to a knowledge of genuine Christian fellowship, so surely must we be overwhelmed by a great disillusionment with others, with Christians in general, and, if we are fortunate, with ourselves.

> By sheer grace, God will not permit us to live even for a brief period in a dream world. He does not abandon us to those rapturous experiences and lofty moods that come over us like a dream. God is not a God of the emotions but the God of truth. Only that fellowship which faces such disillusionment, with all its unhappy and ugly aspects, begins to be what it should be in God's sight, begins to grasp in faith the promise that

is given to it. The sooner the shock of disillusionment comes to an individual and to a community the better for both. A community which cannot bear and cannot survive such a crisis, which insists upon keeping its illusion when it should be shattered, permanently loses in that moment the promise of Christian community. Sooner or later it will collapse. Every human wish dream that is injected into the Christian community is a hindrance to genuine community and must be banished if genuine community is to survive. He who loves his dream of a community more than the Christian community itself becomes a destroyer of the latter, even though his personal intentions may be ever so honest and earnest and sacrificial.[4]

As a community, we did not fail our friend who committed adultery; the dream of community failed us all. Thankfully, as Bonhoeffer put it, "God will not permit us to live even for a brief period in a dream world." During the month Chad and Mark died, I saw remarkable examples of authentic Christian community among my friends. However, as with our local community, we recognized that we still underestimate the gravity of what it means to be a part of the people of God. This is not an outpost for disaffected church leaders. This is not a think-tank to discover new church planting methods. This is not an excuse to drink beer, discuss theology, and gripe about the institutional church. The reality of Christian community is much more frightening.

Authentic Christian community is not built, it is received. Bonhoeffer says:

> Because God has already laid the only foundation (Christ) of our fellowship, because God has bound us together in one body with other Christians in Jesus Christ, long before we entered into common

life with them, we enter into that common life not as demanders but as thankful recipients.[5]

Christian brotherhood is not an ideal which we must realize; it is rather a reality created by God in Christ in which we may participate.[6]

Once there was a woman who had a small garden in her backyard. She was young, innocent, a newlywed. This was her and her husband's first home, complete with a porch swing and white picket fence. It was a large home; large enough to build a family over many years. She had dreams for this family. Soon her house would be filled with the noise and activity of her children and her children's children. One day she went out to her garden and planted a seed. It was an insignificant planting—no one noticed what she was doing or what she placed in the ground. It could have been just more corn or cabbage or tomatoes, an organism that would grow for a season, produce fruit, and wither and die by fall. But this was a mustard seed—tiny, fragile, inconsequential—yet held in its genes the potential energy of a life that would far surpass any corn, cabbage, or tomato plant. Planting such a seed is a risky proposition. Would it survive animals and bugs, be wilted by the sun, dry out from lack of water, or withstand its first harsh winter? Against those odds, the seed grew into a small sapling. The small sapling then grew sturdier, progressively making its presence known, but always with the unobtrusive nature of slow organic growth. Eventually, it became a tree, and the children would play beneath the same branches where birds had made their nests. The woman grew old with the tree and one day passed on the house to another family and another generation.

Despite our efforts, the community of God grows and matures into the tree he desires to provide shade for his children. We enter this community, this family, just as the disciples entered Jesus' family in the first century. We do not deserve to be a part of this family, to have brothers and sisters that love us in spite of our flaws. They do not deserve our love either. However, that is how this family operates. There is no other way. There is no dream, no strategy, no program for making this family work. God's only way is love. And love is the most counter-cultural, most *subversive*, force known to man on planet earth.

Chapter Five

Christian Subversion

I chose to do some writing tonight at the local Panera Bread restaurant, munching on a cookie, and sipping the dark roast. There is nothing unusual about my presence here. Certainly it is quite common these days to see someone with a laptop open, using the free wifi, and listening to his or her mp3 player. I could be doing anything: working on a school paper, planning my investments, checking the basketball scores, chatting with my brother, but that is not my purpose. I am, unbeknownst to these other happy people present, a subversive of the most dangerous kind. My interest is nothing less than a complete upheaval of the values that many of these people hold dear, to see those values sabotaged by the wild and wonderful reign of Jesus Christ.

What Is Church?

South Florida is not a coffee culture, so there are not many places to park your laptop with a good cup of coffee on a Saturday evening. Panera Bread, in my humble opinion, has beat on many fronts the Evil Empire (need I mention the name that starts with an S and ends with an 'ucks'?). Their coffee blends do not taste burnt, their cookies and pastries are better, they don't charge for wifi, they have fresh food, and I have never once had to wait in line while some oblivious individual orders their triple mocha skim-milk venti frappuccino. Strictly speaking as a consumer, Panera Bread makes me happy. Everything about the place screams, "Sit down and take a load off. Eat some carb-laden French bread and have a bowl of the broccoli cheddar. Converse with your friends, drink coffee, take home a few brownies… live a little." As a matter of fact, if I were a single man, I might eat at Panera Bread several times a week.

Such has become the American way of life. We find something we like; we overdose on it until the law of diminishing returns rears its ugly head. In the midst of our search for the next high, we become incapable of being confronted with anything inconvenient or painful. We forget that once there was no such thing as Panera Bread or Starbucks or Pottery Barn. Our story as consumers has become a story of accelerating technology, hyper-efficiency, and stifling homogeneity. These and other values have usurped every rivaling story in this culture, including the Christian story. Many churches have attempted to walk the tightrope by making every effort to present the way of Christ without offending those values too deeply, even in some cases using those values as a means to discipleship.

However, if it has not been made clear up to this point, getting more people in your church is not the measure of success in the kingdom of God or what it means to *reach people for Jesus.* Neither is external conformity to biblical values, doing church like it says in the New Testament, or voting Republican (or Democrat, for that matter). I believe it is imperative that another path be discovered, one that prophetically challenges those values as well as our American cultural identity as consumers. It does not look like fundamentalism, railroading others into a systematic worldview of do's and don'ts. It does not look like isolationism, diving beneath the covers in a futile attempt to insulate the faithful from the surrounding wickedness. It also does not look like nihilism, decreeing everything in its path corrupt and leaving no hope for reconstruction. No, this path has everything to do with announcing the accessibility of the *kingdom among us* and demonstrating its concrete reality through word and deed.

A good biblical model for this kind of announcement can be found in the prophet Jeremiah. The numbness produced by our culture's values can only be broken by an authentic expression of emotions that everyone has but no one is willing to acknowledge. Walter Bruggemann presents a portrait of Jeremiah's ministry that stands in contrast to more familiar ones. Living amongst a people who could not and did not want to see that the end was near, he became the symbol of a grieving nation that could not grieve:

> [Jeremiah] is a paradigm for those who address the numb and denying posture of people who do not want to know what they have or what their neighbors have. Jeremiah is frequently misunderstood as a doomsday spokesman or a pitiful man who had a grudge and sat around crying; but his public and personal grief was for another reason and served another purpose. Jeremiah embodies the alternative consciousness of Moses in the face of the denying king...He articulated what the community had to deny in order to continue the self-deception of achievable satiation...In his grieving,

What Is Church?

> Jeremiah asked only that the royal community face up
> to its real experience, so close to the end. What both
> prophet and king knew was that to experience that
> reality was in fact to cease to be king.[1]

In other words, Jeremiah's prophetic vocation was to
do for the people of Judea what they could not do—confess
that their prosperity was not infinite and that they would
in fact lose their identity, and indeed their own lives, under
the judgment of God. The king in Jeremiah's time wished
to *live in an uninterrupted eternal now*. But God's people have
always and will always live by God's timetable. The king
and his establishment seek to live in a world where every
question is answered, every concern managed, and every
pain comforted. But instead, the prophet asks,

> Is there no balm in Gilead?
>> Is there no physician there?
>> Why then is there no healing
>> for the wound of my people?
> O, that my head were a spring of water
>> and my eyes a fountain of tears!
>> I might weep day and night
>> for the slain of my people.
> O, that I had in the desert
>> a lodging place for travelers,
>> so that I might leave my people
>> and go away from them;
>> for they are all adulterers,
>> a crowd of unfaithful people. (Jeremiah 8.22-9.2)

The prophet is willing to confront the questions that
have no easy answers, because that is the only path that
might break the numbness. "Now it is time not for answers
but for questions that defy answers because the royal

answering service no longer functions. Answers from that source presume control and symmetry. And that is gone. ^{"2} With the establishment's set of answers lying in the gutter, the prophet stands as a paradigmatic witness to the perilous narrow road, which is the only way forward.

However, the challenge before us is not simply discerning that a narrow road needs to be followed. It is fully grasping what might be required of us to take our first steps. The danger here is jumping to the wrong conclusions when presented with the ministry of Jesus. Will we try to make him King without fully understanding his kingdom? Will we decide that his ways are too subtle, too indirect, and attempt to bring his kingdom through brute force? Will we determine that isolation from the world is the only means to respond to his call to become a renewed people? In order to fully hear and respond to what Jesus might say to us as Western Christians in the twenty-first century, we need to discover a new context for approaching him.

First, we cannot begin the conversation as guardians of a utopian dream, such as an attempt to sustain a *Christian Nation*. One need only to look at our European neighbors to discover how marginalized Christianity will quickly become in North America. Many would view this as a cop-out, resigning the nation to a godless future. However, I would offer the following as a few simple tests to determine if the current models for keeping America a Christian Nation are working. Drive down to your local city or county government building and stand in line at the tax assessor's office. Or, go to any large retailer on December 26 and wait at the returns desk. Observe the number of people who are demonstrating patience or kindness to their neighbor. Attend a meeting for your neighborhood homeowner's association and take note of who is able to control their anger when something happens that threatens their privacy or costs them a few extra dollars. Walk along a south Florida beach on a hot summer afternoon and see how many young women are dressed modestly or how many young men show respect and restraint when an attractive woman walks by. Visit a nursing home and poll how often families come to visit their fathers and mothers or when the last time a nursing home worker was sincerely thanked by a family member for their difficult work.

It would not take an observant person long to discern that the teachings of Jesus are not practiced with much regularity in the course of everyday life. You might object by saying, "But look at the teen pregnancy rates, they are going down!" Or, "My church is busting out the seams with new members and all sorts of great ministry!" Or, "The president is a Christian! Surely God must be happy about that!" Jesus did not die on the cross and rise from the dead to lower a statistic, build a successful religious organization, or ensure that the head of the country says the right things to his evangelical constituency. God's plan was, is, and will continue to be renewal of the cosmos through the restoration of the human heart. Dallas Willard describes it in this way:

> The revolution of Jesus is in the first place and continuously a revolution of the human heart or spirit. It did not and does not proceed by means of the formation of social institutions and laws, the outer forms of our existence, intending that these would then impose a good order of life upon people who come under their power. Rather, his is a revolution of character, which proceeds by changing people from the inside through ongoing personal relationship to God in Christ and to one another. It is one that changes their ideas, beliefs, feelings, and habits of choice, as well as their bodily tendencies and social relations. It penetrates to the deepest layers of their soul.[3]

What Is Church?

Revolution is a word that can raise eyebrows if spoken in the right context. I do not suppose that Dallas Willard was put on a watch list by the FBI after writing *Renovation of the Heart*. That being said, it does not appear that the Romans or the Jewish leaders were all that concerned about Jesus' followers after he was executed by Pilate either. Yet, after a few short years it was said about them,

> These men who have turned the world upside down have come here also, and Jason has received them, and they are all acting against the decrees of Caesar, saying that there is another king, Jesus. And the people and the city authorities were disturbed when they heard these things. (Acts 17.6–8, *English Standard Version*)

How did a few, mostly uneducated men and women, crossing sociological, religious, and geographic boundaries with no political power, turn the world upside down? Was it just a miraculous, unrepeatable act of the Spirit? Or, was this exactly what Jesus expected from his disciples throughout the ages until the consummation of his kingdom?

When Jesus sent out his disciples to minister for the first time, he gave them some very simple yet direct instructions:

> Do not go among the Gentiles or enter any town of the Samaritans. Go rather to the lost sheep of Israel. As you go, preach this message: 'The kingdom of heaven is near.' Heal the sick, raise the dead, cleanse those who have leprosy, drive out demons. Freely you have received, freely give. Do not take along any gold or silver or copper in your belts; take no bag for the journey, or extra tunic, or sandals or a staff; for the worker is worth his keep.
>
> Whatever town or village you enter, search for

some worthy person there and stay at his house until you leave. As you enter the home, give it your greeting. If the home is deserving, let your peace rest on it; if it is not, let your peace return to you. (Matthew 10.5–13)

Jesus told his disciples to go out preaching and demonstrating the presence and availability of his kingdom. They would not need a lot of equipment or money to do their kingdom work. They were the equipment. He sent them to the people of Israel, where "the harvest was plentiful but the workers are few" (Matthew 9.37). He also instructed them to simply find a normal, honest person to stay with and minister around. Their work was with the ordinary Jewish citizen, the everyday Joe. No pretense. No fluff. Just the message of the kingdom and the power of the Spirit.

Recently I had the opportunity to preach at a small church in southern Peru while on a trip to visit some missionary friends. The pastor, a former police chief, showed me around the church facility. They had a full worship band complete with two guitars, a bass, drums, and keyboard. All of their band members were young and attractive, dressed in color-coordinated dresses and suits. They had a video projector for the song lyrics and church announcements. The walls of the building were adorned with posters showing the different programs offered by the church and how to become involved in ministry. There was even a poster showing Rick Warren's famous *bases* from the book *Purpose Driven Church*. They were, at least by the standards of most American churches, doing the right things to get people in the door and keeping them there. However, earlier that week I had spent an evening with their small group leaders and our missionary friends. After a long meeting where they asked us many questions about our church and ministry methods, someone from our team asked them, "So what do you see God doing in your church? How is he at work among you?" They could not answer the question. Their effort at mimicking the American vision of a successful church was admirable, but they were oblivious to God's action in their midst.

This is indicative of what is happening in the church all over the world. Enormous sums of money are being spent in order to attract the consumer to a Sunday service, while more is being embezzled by church staff and treasurers than is being directed towards world missions.[4] If that is not enough to call for a revolution, I do not know what it will take. This revolution begins with Jesus and the example of his revolutionaries throughout the ages. He is asking us to first take a look inside, and trust him with the restoration of our own hearts. Are we willing to walk the narrow path, to have our character reshaped by the Spirit in order to freely and cheerfully live as he taught his disciples to live? This will, no doubt, result in the death of our desire to get our own way, including our aspirations to be successful, of course. We will resist this transformation and will find few companions and advocates. This, again, is nothing new. A revolution does not begin out of a place of power or among people who are enamored with the latest fad. This is the work of subversives.

Christian Subversion 101

Subversive is an odd word to associate with Christianity, but that is only because of its uses in recent world history. Webster's defines *subvert*, "to overturn or overthrow from the foundation." Its origin is Latin, "subvertere, literally, to turn from beneath." Eugene Peterson describes subversion in this way:

Three things are implicit in subversion. One, the status quo is wrong and must be overthrown if the world is going to be livable. It is so deeply wrong that repair work is futile. The world is, in the word insurance agents use to designate our wrecked cars, totaled.

Two, there is another world aborning that is livable. Its reality is no chimera. It is in existence, though not visible. Its character is known. The subversive does not operate out of a utopian dream but out of a conviction of the nature of the real world.

Three, the usual means by which one kingdom is thrown out and another put in its place—military force or democratic elections—are not available. If we have neither a preponderance of power nor a majority of votes, we begin searching for other ways to effect change. We discover the methods of subversion. We find and welcome allies.[5]

The mission of the Christian subversive is not to bring the kingdom of God from without; it is to release the kingdom from within. Subversives do not reach outside people and encourage them to come in. Subversives live and do their work *undercover* where the world lives and breathes. Their goal is not escapism (trying to build a Christian utopia), but to show people how they can lay hold of life as God intended and develop communities where that life flourishes.

The Christian subversive understands that the status quo and its methods are false. It is constantly interacting with people at work, in the grocery store, or at home who are all in the prison of the dominant kingdom. These prisoners are quite happy in their assumed reality, especially the ones

who have amassed quite a kingdom of wealth. But some
secretly ask the question, "Is this really all there is to life?"
The Christian subversive's answer is not merely to inform
them about the real kingdom, but to invite them to become
participants in a whole new reality. Even getting some to
believe that this reality exists will be difficult. Most will
be satisfied that they will one day see this kingdom, but
only after they are dead. Some will reject this kingdom and
its wounded King and simply carry on with their favorite
agenda. For those who decide to enter this kingdom now, a
training program will be necessary. Training will be unique
for each person and culture and cannot be rushed or broken
down into principles or a program. Remember, the kingdom
of God deals with every aspect of life. This training might
just take a lifetime. At all points in the process, the Christian
subversive is receiving his or her direction and power from
Jesus himself through the Spirit. Again, there is absolutely
no budget or program necessary to accomplish this work. In
fact, in this time we live, refusal to assign a budget or create
a system for ministry may be one of the most subversive
things we can do.

The chief aim of a Christian subversive is to train other
subversives, which is the Great Commission in a nutshell.

> God authorized and commanded me to commission
> you: Go out and train everyone you meet, far and
> near, in this way of life, marking them by baptism
> in the threefold name: Father, Son, and Holy Spirit.
> Then instruct them in the practice of all I have
> commanded you. I'll be with you as you do this, day
> after day after day, right up to the end of the age.
> (Matthew 28.18–20, *The Message*)

It does not appear that Jesus thought this task would

start and end with the first disciples. He had Paul and
Timothy in mind as much as James and Peter. He had
Augustine and Patrick in mind as much as you or me.

So what are our tools? Where do we begin in this
training? How do we train others? What does it mean for
the church? In the next chapter, I will begin to explore the
"What if?" of becoming an apprentice of Jesus. But first
I would like to suggest how Christian subversives might
practice ways the local church has both maintained its
identity as the People of God and been a prophetic voice
in culture throughout its history. These ways, of course,
center around Jesus and the way he trained his disciples.
He taught them to heal the sick, cast out demons, raise the
dead, and preach the message of the kingdom. He taught
them to baptize in his name, welcoming new disciples into
the family of God. And he taught them to remember his
death through the Lord's Supper and look forward to the
fulfillment of the kingdom and the resurrection.

Communion Reloaded

If you are anything like me, your experience with the
Lord's Supper in church has been unremarkable at best.
For most people who have grown up in the evangelical
tradition, you probably recall the silver trays being passed
around with little plastic cups of grape juice and stale matzo.
An admonition to spend time in reflection and repentance
was given, the passage from the last supper narrative was
read, and then you took the elements with your family.
Occasionally this pattern was repeated during a special
occasion—Good Friday, Christmas Eve, at a special time
of corporate prayer, or after a baptism—that possibly held
greater significance than the monthly observance. But
regardless of the occasion, the theological and experiential

weight the Lord's Supper bore was primarily about asking forgiveness for your own sin and remembering Jesus' death and sacrifice on the cross.

Certainly there can be nothing wrong with remembering Jesus' death on the cross and taking occasion to reflect on the areas where we fall short and are in need of restoration. However, given both the theological and prophetic weight of this meal that Jesus gave to his disciples, it is necessary to ask some hard questions of our practices and see where we are led.

There are two questions that stand out as commensurate to our task. First, has the practice of the Lord's Supper as evangelicals have practiced it in recent times been in any way reductionistic? Second, is there anything we can learn from other Christian faith traditions that would lead us to a richer experience of worship and prophetic edge? I think the obvious answer to both questions is 'yes', but equally obvious is the need for help discovering 'how' and 'what' we need to learn.

Before we can address these questions, however, a more fundamental question needs to be asked: Why even bother with celebrating the Lord's Supper? That might be a little shocking to some, but for others it might be refreshing to hear someone actually ask it honestly. For those of us who have spent the past years unpacking and repacking our formation as Christians (or human beings for that matter), it is a natural and fitting question. Why do we spend the time putting on this little show with bread and wine once a week or month? Is it *really* that important in the scheme of things as followers of Jesus and a community of faith?

Of course, it is tempting to just say, "Well, we do it because Jesus said so." That is not a bad answer, but excuse me for mimicking my three-year-old son, *why* did Jesus say so? Did he arbitrarily choose bread and wine? Why not meat and potatoes? Water and wood? Figs and mustard seeds? Did he really expect generations of his followers to do the *same thing* and read the *same words* to commemorate his death? Isn't it just more important to love God and your neighbor and try to follow Jesus' commands? After all, Jesus certainly did not anticipate his church inventing the single-use, vacuum-sealed, disposable communion container, did he? With all the theological reduction, practical weirdness, and just plain silliness the church gets itself into, why bother?

Good question. But it brings up an even deeper question that has to be posed. Maybe we should forget all about this church stuff and just focus on being better people. Certainly Jesus spent a lot of time demonstrating his distaste for the religious posturing of his day. He did not seem to care about pomp and ceremony, services and structure. But did he envision a social club for Christian spirituality that dabbles in following Jesus like you would dabble in organic gardening? Or did he envision a harrowing and gut-level journey to discover a place in the renewed people of God? I have to believe it was the latter. The Church, for all its bumps and bruises, somehow always finds its compass pointing back to Jesus and his kingdom project. Concerning the Lord's Supper, I want to introduce a few ideas that may help answer the *why should we bother* question. First of all, in case you haven't noticed, eating is a pretty important activity in the Bible. From the apple in the Garden to Jesus eating with prostitutes and tax collectors, food carries biblical weight. When Jesus feasted with sinners, it was not just to tick off the Pharisees. His feasts revealed something of kingdom reality.

> You'll watch outsiders stream in from east, west, north, and south and sit down at the table of God's kingdom. And all the time you'll be outside looking in--and wondering what happened. This is the Great Reversal: the last in line put at the head

of the line, and the so-called first ending up last. (Luke 13.29–30, *The Message*)

Throughout history, eating together has been a sign of acceptance and friendship. Jesus demonstrated his friendship with the worst of the sinners of his day, but he looked forward to a time when anyone who called him Lord would sit down for the Feast of Feasts.

But why did he ordain this particular meal, the bread and wine, to be repeated by his followers? A starting place might be to look at what this simple meal would mean to a first-century Jew. The Jews in Jesus' day inhabited the land promised by God to Abraham, but in a real sense were still in exile. Dominated by Rome, factions of Jewish hierarchy fought over competing visions of how Israel might in fact become, once again, ruled by Yahweh and Yahweh alone. Was it by defeating Rome militarily and reclaiming political power? Was it by escaping into the wilderness and waiting until God destroyed their enemies? Or was it by becoming slick compromisers and grasping for every ounce of power that could be sucked from Rome's grasp? To put it succinctly, Israel was undergoing an identity crisis of national proportions.

This was a world where symbols were much more integral to life than flags or monuments. For the Jews, the Temple carried the ultimate symbolic and existential weight. It was, after all, where God chose to set up shop with his people. Never mind that some Jews were less than thrilled that it was built by the murderous Herod and certainly was a shadow of Solomon's glorious structure. The Temple was the center of Jewish religion, politics, economy, military, and culture.

So consider the story of Jesus cleansing the Temple. Was this act just to demonstrate Jesus' zeal for God and righteousness? If so, why couldn't he have done the same thing at the downtown market? No, it was a direct challenge, an arrow in the heart if you will, to the prevailing idea of what it meant to be the people of God, to be Israel. N. T. Wright in *The Challenge of Jesus* reveals:

> His attitude to the Temple was not 'this institution needs reforming,' nor 'the wrong people are running the place,' nor yet 'piety can function elsewhere too.' His deepest belief regarding the Temple was eschatological—the time had come for God to judge the entire institution. It had come to symbolize the injustice that characterized the society on the inside and on the outside, the rejection of the vocation to be the light of the world, the city set on a hill that would draw to itself all the peoples of the world.[6]

Later that week, Jesus would gather with his disciples to celebrate the Passover meal, another intensely symbolic activity for the Jews. The Passover meal held double meaning for first century Jews. It certainly recalled their deliverance out of Egypt by the hand of God, but it also looked forward to their own final redemption, the coming of the kingdom and defeat of their enemies. Jesus, in celebrating this meal with his band of followers and using the elemental bread and wine, revealed his intentions to take Israel's fate on his own shoulders. Instead of blood on the doorposts and dead firstborn sons, there would be a body broken and blood spilled on a cross.

> In this context the words that he spoke [during the last supper] suggest that Jesus was deliberately evoking the whole exodus-tradition and indicating that the hope of Israel would now come true in and through his own death. His death, he seems to be saying, must be seen within the context of the larger story of YHWH's redemption of Israel; more specifically, it would be

the central and climactic moment toward which that story had been moving. Those who shared the meal with him were the people of the renewed covenant, the people who received 'the forgiveness of sins,' that is, the end of exile. Grouped around him, they constituted the true eschatological Israel.[7]

When we take the Lord's Supper, we are not just agreeing to a theological principle or performing a dutiful act of remembrance like laying flowers on a grave. The Lord's Supper is a many-layered subversive and prophetic act that declares once and for all—the exile of God's people is over. The kingdom of God has come and will culminate in a final feast where all the friends of Jesus, regardless of class, race, gender, or nationality will sit at his table. The People of God is not a proud, pure, triumphant nation, but a rag-tag band of sinners living in the grace of God. In our feasting, fellowship, and dogged dependence on Jesus, we proclaim his grace to the world.

Come on in, Boys, the Water's Fine

Well, that's it, boys, I've been redeemed! The preacher washed away all my sins and transgressions. It's the straight-and-narrow from here on out and heaven everlasting is my reward![8]

Delmar could not have said it any better—"Come on in, boys, the water's fine!" This is the bliss of baptism, stretching from John the Baptist in the Jordan to now. I was baptized when I was very young, in our pool at home by my Dad surrounded by my family. I am thankful for my upbringing and early education in what it means to follow Jesus and there is no doubt that I made the decision to trust Jesus and be baptized on my own without excessive coaching from my parents. However, if there is one regret I have about the actual event of my baptism, it is that other members of God's family were not present. It is this communal and familial reality to baptism—becoming part of God's people—which is the most critical to our current discussion.

Before I get ahead of myself, it might be helpful to level the playing field a bit in light of the controversies the wider church has regarding baptism. First of all, if we can agree that becoming a Christian means a whole bunch more than getting into heaven when we die, then many of the arguments about whether you get *saved* at baptism or before or after just are not that important. Rather, baptism becomes more indicative of what following Jesus is about from start to finish—death and resurrection. Just as Jesus died and rose again, we are told, "If anyone would come after me, he must deny himself and take up his cross and follow me," and given the promise "…in the twinkling of an eye…the dead will be raised imperishable, and we will be changed." We live in the tension between those two realities, between Good Friday and Resurrection Sunday. Thankfully, we are baptized into good company—Jesus and the saints who have gone before us. Inagrace Dietterich in the book *Missional Church, A Vision for the Sending of the Church in North America* describes baptism in this way:

> The cross and resurrection break the universal reign of sin and death and begin a new reign of forgiveness and freedom. In Jesus Christ the depth of divine love, the seriousness of human sin, the power of evil and the faithfulness of God are revealed. As incorporation into the crucified and risen Lord, baptism is not simply turning over a new leaf, or adopting a few new beliefs, but a matter of life and death: 'Baptism is a training in dying—specifically to sin, to the old self—so that people may be brought to newness of life.'[9]

What Is Church?

Newness of life implies that we are introduced into a new way of looking at the world, a kingdom-of-God way. After all, we aren't simply carried off into heaven or given our resurrection bodies the minute we come out of the water. We are still living in the world, same as before. Baptism introduces us to a new context for living that is dominated by Jesus and his way of life rather than the world and its way of life. Dietterich says:

> Baptism plunges believers into a situation where the old (the power of all that is hostile to the reign of God) has passed away (2 Cor. 5.17), although the old can still afflict, perplex, persecute, or strike down (2 Cor. 4.7-18). The present reality of alienation, brokenness, and injustice demonstrates the gap and tension between our contemporary world and the fullness of the reign of God. Because baptism links believers with the death as well as the resurrection of Jesus Christ, missional communities participate in his suffering and self-giving ministry. They are called to live into their baptism, to learn daily how to die and thus how to live. They are summoned to offer their lives and their service in the fulfillment of God's ministry of reconciliation. As such, baptism goes far beyond the private salvation of the individual soul or the isolated moment of baptism. It forms a new humanity by incorporating believers into the body of Jesus Christ and beginning their formation as a missionary people.[10]

I love the phrase *live into their baptism.* It is so simple, but could be a wonderful training tool for any follower of Jesus. In the midst of the church's endless debates about the mechanics of baptism, the reality of what the act teaches us about life in Christ gets lost. Eugene Peterson eloquently writes, "Baptism is at one and the same time death and resurrection, a renunciation and an embrace." They left their nets...and followed him. Repent...and believe. Put off your old self...and put on the new self. This is the life of the baptized.

But as I alluded to above, the life of the baptized is not lived in isolation. The wonder of baptism that was perhaps lost on me in my pool at home was that I was being invited into a family much larger than my own (or even my church for that matter). Paul routinely impressed upon the early church that—in spite of their differences—they were one family, an adopted family.

> You are all sons of God through faith in Christ Jesus, for all of you who were baptized into Christ have clothed yourselves with Christ. There is neither Jew nor Greek, slave nor free, male nor female, for you are all one in Christ Jesus. If you belong to Christ, then you are Abraham's seed, and heirs according to the promise." (Galatians 3.26–29)

Rodney Clapp continues with this idea:

[Paul] reminds believers that they have a new identity because they have been baptized into Christ and adopted as his sisters and brothers. When children are adopted they take on new parents, new siblings, new names, new inheritances—in short, a new culture. And those who have been baptized into Christ, according to Paul, have been adopted by God. This baptism means that Christians' new parent is God the Father. Their new siblings are other Christians. Their new name or most functional identity is simply Christians—those who know Jesus as Lord and determiner of their existence. Their new inheritance is freedom and the bountiful resources of community. Their new culture, or comprehensive way of life, is the church. It is in this profound sense that Paul can speak of conversion and baptism creating a new person—even a new world (2 Cor. 5.17).[11]

Baptism invites us to become part of God's family, his adopted sons and daughters. There is a profound equality and unity that results from this adoption (or at least, that's what Jesus prayed for—John 17.20–21). In a strange way, our own sons and daughters become our brothers and sisters, who like us have been adopted, forgiven, healed, set free. We lay down the human need to control one another, as we each have one Father, one King, one Lord. We can no longer live only for ourselves, for we have acknowledged publicly that we've pretty much made a mess of things trying to get our own way up until now. And, we continue to remind ourselves in stubborn worship and through messy relationships that Jesus is real and he is zealously intent on making the world right again.

Embracing the Whole Ministry of Jesus

In many circles, Bob Ekblad would be considered a left of left-wing liberal. He studied theology in France with his wife and spent years in Honduras and now in Washington state ministering to the poor.[12] But in 2003, he had a profound experience with the Holy Spirit at a pastor's retreat in Toronto which revolutionized his ministry. Now, physical healing, inner healing, and deliverance ministry have become a routine part of Bob's ongoing work. What happened to Bob is a stark example of how God is blurring the lines we have traditionally drawn for ourselves in ministry.

Ekblad's message is simple: vast portions of the church

and ministries that support bringing justice to the world, ministry to the poor, and advocacy for the weak have divorced the demonstration of God's power—specifically healing, deliverance, and the supernaturally prophetic—from their theology and praxis. His argument is not primarily an academic one, although he is certainly capable of making a well-informed biblical argument for the necessity of integrating the charismatic and social justice streams. Rather, he has had profound first-hand experience, both of God powerfully intervening in his own life and in the lives of those his ministry has touched for the past few years.

Recently I was at a conference with some friends and cohorts and had the opportunity to hear Ekblad speak. After telling his story, he invited people to come forward and receive whatever God wanted to give—empowerment, encouragement, healing, release. I was able to participate in some of the ministry during that time and had the pleasure of watching the Spirit touch a few people in a profound way. Later, during the question and answer session, many shared both their excitement and curiosity, as well as their skepticism and pain associated with previous negative experiences. One question that arose several times dealt with the issue of suffering. Namely, what do we do if people do not get healed or delivered or touched? Ekblad told many stories of healings occurring from serious and life-threatening illnesses. Yet many have had experiences where someone was not healed or the person ministering was discovered to be a fake. This incongruence justifiably produces some difficult questions, but where should those questions leave us?

On the flight home, I was replaying in my mind some of the responses and questions from that conversation. It dawned on me that much of what was said was rooted firmly in a Western, rationalistic worldview. Upon reflection, this honestly surprised and disturbed me. Here are people who for the most part have identified themselves with God's kingdom and aligned themselves with his purposes. They are reflecting on the implications of living as a disciple of Jesus in America in all aspects of life. They are experimenting with new forms of church and extremely committed to seeing justice, mercy, and healing come to the *least of these.* They are also aware that traditional evangelical readings of scripture fall short when it comes to awakening the average Christian to the socially prophetic realities of God's rule on earth. Yet, when confronted with a person who shares all of these concerns, but is actively participating in the demonstration of God's power as a normal element of day-in-day-out ministry—of life, really—they end up sounding more like functional cessationists than people convinced that God as Spirit is working in the world to make things right, in spite of any rational data they might have to the contrary.

Of course, to be fair, it is not like I stand here as someone flowing in the supernatural power of God as naturally as hopping on my bike and riding to the grocery store. However, to whom much has been given, much will be required. I have had some wonderful training and experiences related to healing, deliverance, and the prophetic, specifically. Those experiences and examples compel me to keep seeking and experimenting in our current context. I am also interested to *practice* with others who have the same hunger for God's presence. This is, naturally, not meant to exclude the expressions of Christian life we have been tasting of and growing in—worship, contemplative practices, one-anothering, sharing of each other's burdens, becoming more acquainted with God's Story, and interpreting the scriptures as a community. It is simply recognition that God is spirit, and so are we. The *unseen* nature of God's kingdom is not just that we do not fully see how he is setting the world right or will set the world right one day. It is that he operates *both* at a level we can see—within the relationships and earthly contexts we find ourselves in—*and* in the heavenly realm of spirit and spiritual power. It is the latter that the western, rationalistic worldview is woefully ill equipped to understand or deal with.

If the emerging church (however you wish to define it) is to truly become an agent for change in Western Christianity, and hopefully a unifying force, then it must be willing to lay down its pride regarding the supernatural. No, we cannot understand why God heals some people and does not heal others. In the exploding church of Africa, when a child is dying of AIDS or a young woman is suffering from a tumor and has neither the means or opportunity to have it surgically removed, there is not much discussion why God might heal one but not the other. Both are prayed for and guess what…often they are both healed. Our questions are valid, but they should not paralyze us from joining in on what God is doing. We have not shied away from the complications related to the huge, cultural shifts occurring around us and the impact those shifts are having on church. Likewise, we should not shy away from diving into what God is doing, both seen and unseen.

In the end, this question must be dealt with corporately as God's people in community. We will not make headway by sitting alone with our questions or passively ignoring portions of our discipleship that do not make rational sense. Experience proves that people who truly follow Jesus will be given the necessary discernment and wisdom to grow in areas that just don't fit in our western framework. But, we have to be willing to trust each other, and more importantly, trust God's Spirit. After all, if following Jesus requires us to take up our cross daily, to deny ourselves, to *lose control*, then trusting God's Spirit to teach us all everything about his nature and his power should not be any more of a stretch than trusting that he will one day raise us all from the dead. The fact is, learning to minister as Jesus did does require training, but it is not the stuff of experts or the specially *gifted*. We see the up-front personalities of the charismatic movement and either reject their weirdness or determine that we'll never be able to minister with the same confidence they seem to exude. Regardless, none of it seems to be transferable to daily life and our unfamiliarity begins to breed contempt. Soon, we determine that if God wants to do anything out of the ordinary, that is his business and we'll leave that kind of stuff to the weirdos.

Subversive Christians will find another way—one that is not hyped or weird, that stays away from excesses or confusion. More importantly, they will look for how God wants to reveal his power among the ordinary circumstances of life. This will take humility, patience, and trust that God is capable of leading and teaching his children, even in ways that seem uncomfortable or unfamiliar. In order for that to occur, however, the community must begin to see itself as something other than a loose collection of people that don't *fit* in church anymore. But it also can't be full of self-justification, where the market has supposedly been cornered on *doing church* and the boundaries of acceptable practice are encased in concrete. In order to become whole, to be baptized fully in the *Streams of Living Water* as Foster describes, the community must look to another way of learning entirely—a framework that invites Jesus to take his rightful place as rabbi, teacher—becoming his apprentices.

Chapter Six

Apprentices of Jesus

Apprenticeship is a dying art. Most job training has been whittled down to a few years in college and an endless sea of *continuing education* you attend in the working world. This was not the case in the first century, or even just a century ago. Most occupations demanded that a young person seeking employment undergo a long period of shadow work—watching, listening, and copying a master.

This was the way Jesus taught the first disciples and he is still teaching today. It should be obvious that becoming a Christian is not about taking the right Bible classes so you can get the right answers. Rather, following Jesus is like deciding to enter into a new line of work that requires the dedication of your whole being. That is why the language of apprenticeship is helpful in developing an imagination for this life. Apprentices of Jesus submit themselves to an intensive shadow work. They watch: "So they pulled their boats up on shore, left everything and followed him" (Luke 5.11). They listen: "Anyone who listens to my teaching and obeys me is wise, like a person who builds a house on solid rock" (Matthew 7.24). They copy: "...anyone who has faith in me will do what I have been doing. He will do even greater things than these...." (John 14.12)

People who decide to become apprentices of Jesus will begin a lifelong relationship with the Master and other apprentices. As a community, they will be formed together in the image of the Master. Progressively, apprentices will be able to do what Jesus did, say what Jesus said, think what Jesus thought, as if he were living their life. However, this ability does not come by mere human effort. It is a spiritual transformation of the entire human makeup—heart, thoughts, feelings, body, relationships, and even the soul. Although the primary contributor to this transformation is God, it can only occur if the apprentice intends it to happen. He or she must be willing to learn. Jesus will never force anyone to follow him who does not wish to.

However, apprenticeship to Jesus means not quite knowing what you are getting yourself into. There is an enormous amount of trust involved in following the Master. He calls the shots and you might end up sweeping the floor for a year *or twenty*. When did we ever get the idea that following Jesus was glamorous? Maybe that is what the Christian celebrity of the month is selling, but it is not reality. The beauty of forgiveness, of healing and grace, is often followed by a life filled with mistakes, loneliness, pain, isolation, intimidation, fatigue, and ultimately, death. Not just physical death of course, but *take up your cross and follow me* kind of death.

Following Jesus means learning from him the proper

way to die to experience life. It is spending thirty years in the carpenter's shop and then forty days in the desert. Being baptized by a wild man among the sinners and scum of the land. Collecting a band of nobodies. Getting rejected by family and your own hometown. Traveling the countryside to nowhere towns, having no place to stay, a different bed every night. The consistent clamoring of people asking for you to touch them, to speak to them, to *lead* them, and recognizing that they do not really understand what is happening. Getting bombarded by the religious establishment for every act and suspected of all kinds of heresy. Almost being stoned to death and thrown over a cliff. Rode into town on an ass and celebrated by the people for all the wrong reasons. One precious night with his band of losers, knowing that one of them would betray him to death, then falsely accused and sent off to the government officials. Bound, held, cursed at, beaten to an unrecognizable pulp. Passed over for a murderer. Hung on a tree, killed like an animal, stabbed and left hanging as a public spectacle.

This is the Jesus who we want to follow?

It is not difficult to see that becoming an apprentice of Jesus is an unpopular occupation. There is no one in recent history that I know of who has so accurately both stated this problem and prescribed a solution than Dallas Willard. Early in our journey as a faith community, Willard's thoughts about the kingdom of God and discipleship heavily informed our conversations and sparked further questions. Next to the scriptures, I have probably returned to his book, *The Divine Conspiracy, Rediscovering Our Hidden Life in God,* more times over the past years than I would care to admit. However, I do not intend to repeat his work or others who have devoted their lives and authorship to teaching on discipleship and spiritual formation. My task is demonstrating how the kingdom of God and living as an apprentice of Jesus changes

the rules when it comes to being the church together in
our day and time.

The Well

During the first year together as a faith community,
we often returned to a simple yet challenging question:
What if we thought of ourselves as simply a collection of
people apprenticed to Jesus as Master? The first result of
this was to abandon any plan for what we would become.
For someone trained in the mechanics of church planting,
that was not an easy proposition. Regardless of what they
say, pastors and church planters love to be the person at the
denominational meetings that is touted as an innovator and
has seen their plans come to fruition. The dream, of course,
is to write a book about their success in order to help other
pastors learn and have successful churches on their own.
Our little group knew right out of the gate that we would
never be praised for our *success*.

At some point during that year, we had gathered at Kim
and T Freeman's house for dinner as we did often. There was
little agenda, other than eating too much food and maybe
singing a few songs with the guitar. Later in the evening,
after we laid our newborn son down for bed upstairs, we
spent some time in silence as had become our practice. This
was not a prayer time per se, or in the charismatic tradition
a time for prophetic words. On most occasions, we just kept
our mouths shut and listened. This particular evening, T
read aloud the story from John 6 of the woman at the well.
Here is the story of that night in his own words with some
insight on its meaning for us:

> I had been praying for some insight from God
> specifically for our group, and it might have been
> something we all agreed to seek that night. As others

were praying and sharing, I had a distinct confidence that if I opened the brand-new paperback New Testament sitting in front of me, that I would turn to the story of the woman at the well. I honestly didn't even know the reference to the passage. Sure enough, I opened the book right to that story. I felt like God was highlighting that story as at least a significant part of what we were supposed to hear and be about, but, since others were talking, I figured I'd wait until they were done before reading it aloud. While listening to everybody else, I accidentally let the Bible close again, which was only a problem because I hadn't paid attention to the reference, but I felt like God instantly assured me that I would open right up to it again, which I did.

As we read the passage that night, the impressions I got for our group were several. I've heard it said since that night, that this is one of the theologically richest passages in the Bible. Below is some of what I felt like we were supposed to explore related to this passage now and in the future.

The story is so personal and real and missional, just like we need to be. Jesus is thirsty; the woman is tainted morally, ethnically, and socially, but God initiates with her. He comes in low. She's tired. She wants to talk big religious issues, trying to keep the focus off of her, and Jesus brings it back again and again to himself and to her, in a way customized to her and their conversation. He reveals personal things about her and himself. For example, you don't get Jesus plainly admitting his messiahship very often in scripture. The disciples walk up, adding their awkwardness to this already bizarre moment. The harvest, the mission, is right there in Samaria, an *on the way to somewhere else* place, right under the disciples' noses. But Jesus has to point this fact out to the disciples, and to us.

Along with mission, the story deals with where and how worship happens, which is everywhere, *in spirit and in truth*. Jesus says the Father is seeking people to worship him in that way. As people who are seeking to actually worship God outside of our gatherings (and inside our often unimpressive gatherings), this passage is a big encouragement and guide to us.

Both food and water are talked about, not unimportantly, in this passage. For those of us with longings and holes of the soul, Jesus' words about *never thirsting again* and about his *living water becoming a spring within, welling up to eternal life* are the Gospel itself. After seeing the woman run off to tell her town about him, Jesus is physically satisfied. I don't know if the woman ever got him some water, but he refuses the food the disciples brought him, saying, 'I have food you don't know about...my food is to do the will of the one who sent me and to finish his work.' We need to dive into this reality.

This passage is also about the supremacy of Jesus. The woman asks, 'Are you greater than our father Jacob?' Jesus answer, contrasting Jacob's well with his living water, gives the amazing and currently controversial answer: Yes. Jesus' practical centrality, his messiahship, is the climax of the story. Our culture has the same question for Jesus: 'Are you greater than my current way of doing things? Are you greater than my other authorities?' We need to hear and live his answer.

What Is Church?

Finally, this passage demonstrates how supernatural insight (without any fanfare) is part of the dynamic through which God changes this woman and her town, and centers them on Jesus. It is not the focus of the story, but it is a necessary and ordained part of it that cannot be removed. Neither should we leave or take out such things from among us.

Later that evening, my brother Mark suggested that if we ever decided to name our little church, that *The Well* might be a good fit. A few years ago, we did just that. It is by no means a unique name, as a quick Google search will reveal, but neither are the elements drawn from the story of the woman at the well. What *is* unique to us is the context in which we live, and the people we have crossed paths with up until this point.

South Florida in the first decade of the twenty-first century is a rapidly growing mix of cultures in a prosperous yet over-consumptive environment. We exist because developers destroyed half of the Everglades to provide room for our condos and gated communities. The town I live in, Jupiter, is on the northern border of Palm Beach County, made famous during the *hanging chad* voting scandal of the 2000 presidential election. Jupiter was ground zero for the housing boom a few years ago, and the results of the housing slump are record numbers of foreclosures and financial disasters galore. My wife and I were affected as we were in the middle of selling a house and building a new one when the market went sour. We recently had to sell our old home for far below what we owed. I did not even know what a *short sale* was until all this happened.

Yet, if you drive around our town, it would not be surprising to count as many Mercedes and Jaguars as Fords and Hondas. There is an incredible push to present well in every facet of your life in spite of the financial realities.

This, of course, extends into the church world. A church without the best programs, the latest technology, the most skilled pastors and musicians, and the slickest marketing will simply not stay around for very long.

So where does a group of people begin who desire to be apprenticed to Jesus in a culture like this? In Chapter Two, I discussed what detoxing from church might look like. This is an important step in the process, particularly for those of us who identify with the typical patterns of church that may or may not be helpful in our apprenticeship. However, as with the woman at the well story, there comes a point where the Master leads us into situations where he confronts people in ordinary life—at work, at school, in the grocery store. I am not talking about evangelism specifically; however, this certainly does include telling people about Jesus. This is more about helping us see how God is at work in every situation and he is often most interested in preparing us to be the kinds of people whose "food is to do the will of the one who sent me." This would only happen, of course, if we were intent on learning from Jesus how to actually live like he did. Willard describes this process in the following way:

> The effect of such continuous study under Jesus would naturally be that we learn how to do everything we do 'in the name of the Lord Jesus' (Col. 3.17); that is, on his behalf or in his place; that is, once again, as if he himself were doing it. And of course that means we would learn 'to conform to everything I have commanded you' (Matt. 28.20). In his presence our inner life will be transformed, and we will become the kind of people for whom his course of action is the natural (and supernatural) course of action.[1]

The primary challenge for us in South Florida, and I

would suggest anywhere for that matter, is determining the kind of environment, tools, and leadership required to allow that transformation to take place naturally in a group of Christians. A tall order, you think? Perhaps, but it is a task that is central to unleashing the full weight of God's kingdom on the sleeping giant of the American church. And it begins, predictably, by challenging the two biggest sacred cows of Christendom—preaching and the Sunday service.

The Nutty Professor

Imagine taking a course at a university where the professor lectured once a week for an hour on a topic of his choosing. There was no syllabus, just an enormous, ancient textbook written in multiple dead languages that was at times confusing and extremely difficult to comprehend. Everyone was expected to read the book and get familiar with its contents so the lectures would make more sense. The lectures, predictably, were given with the intent to explain the textbook in greater detail and then prepare the students for future tests.

However, there were several difficulties that were not explained at the outset of the class. First of all, the tests were given at random and on an individual basis. Also, they generally did not relate to the previous lecture and in some cases to any lecture given up to that point. Often the lectures did not follow any particular pattern, but when they did, only a small percentage of people in the class were tested on that specific material. The professor's intent was for the class to be discussing his lectures and the textbook through the week at various times, but that usually did not happen. Sometimes a few people from the class would gather for a study group at one of their homes, but they usually didn't talk about the professor's lectures.

What Is Church?

The generally accepted practice would be for one of the students to take it upon themselves to come up with their own lecture from the textbook and they would discuss that portion.

Some dutifully took notes on the lectures week after week, but became frustrated when they kept failing tests in spite of their diligence. After all, the tests were unpredictable and sometimes dealt with highly specific and advanced material—graduate level work perhaps. These diligent ones tried to study the textbook for themselves and occasionally had a little more success. But others got so wrapped up in their own studies that they began to miss classes and even ignored the tests.

The majority of the students did not take notes or even read the textbook. Most of them were failing tests, or like the self-studiers, missing the tests altogether, but they still came to class week after week to listen to the lectures. The professor, who noticed that his students were struggling on the tests, decided that he probably needed to open another lecture during the week for deeper and further explanation of the textbook. Some of the more conscientious students came to those lectures and added more notes to their notebooks. But the tests kept coming.

The professor decided to open up office hours for his students to come and discuss the material more in depth and to answer specific questions. Some came and took advantage of this opportunity and were able to talk to the professor about why they were failing tests and what they could do to improve. However, others came because the professor was a nice man and would listen to their problems. Pretty soon, the professor had a full schedule of students coming to listen to his advice about anything they felt uncomfortable with about school. The professor would try to help them all, but it was very difficult to give each person exactly what they wanted. Many came back to his office week after week with the same problem, but he had so many people to see that it was impossible to spend the time necessary to help the really hard cases. After a while, the professor was so busy that the people who were coming for help on the tests couldn't even schedule a meeting with him anymore.

Eventually, many of the students began to drop the class. They had found another class where the professor's lectures were much more interesting and more people were signing up to take his classes. They found out quickly that the professor used the same textbook, the tests were still random and difficult, and he was just as busy as the last professor. But he was a much more engaging speaker and appeared to be in tune with their problems at school. Many of the students decided that this just must be what college life is all about—find a good professor to listen to, take good notes, and try to get lucky on a test once in a while.

Beyond Preaching

The story above illustrates what some would argue is a worst case scenario. Surely this is not the norm for most people who attend churches. Remember that I am a self-proclaimed *evangelical poster-child*. For twenty years of my life, I listened to sermons week in and week out. The two men I listened to most often were excellent teachers and were celebrated for their gift in their churches and in their denominations. However, I also lived among the people who made up the churches these men oversaw. Not to take anything away from their gift or their sincerity, but the story above was played out many times over.

It is not that I think one-way communication is evil and preaching sermons is harmful to Christians. It is just that the tests keep coming, and there is nothing anyone can do about it. We need not fool ourselves any longer, what passes for preaching at most churches amounts to either well-meaning yet misplaced attempts at evangelism, messages aimed at improving your quality of life, or pep rally speeches to drum up support for the pastor's vision or the new building program. Not all of these messages are bad. Many of them are given by skilled orators with years of experience and a huge following. However, those represent a very small percentage of the sermons most Christians hear on a weekly basis. Most sermons are given by your average seminary graduate with enough preaching experience to be dangerous.

But the real danger lies not in the delivery or content of most sermons preached, but rather the assumption by most pastors that the sermon is the primary place where Christians learn. There have certainly been times throughout church history where preaching has been indispensable to creating disciples, yet in a culture of Google and Tivo, raw information has never been more accessible or abundant. A good seminary education is literally at your fingertips, if you know where to look. But beyond the necessary context for interpreting the scriptures and becoming acquainted with the history of God's people, there is also ample opportunity to learn a vast array of ministry skills and spiritual disciplines for practical application. If you want to learn about counseling or healing or how to organize a ministry to the homeless, the information and support is within reach. If you want to begin practicing lectio divina, develop a deeper life of prayer, or discover how to control your anger, there are no shortage of resources available.

Of course, there will always be a place for the kerygma, a message spoken to a group of people to accomplish God's purposes. But the idea that this would be the primary component to a person's spiritual development is ridiculous. Some would object, "Doesn't it say in Acts 2.42 that the early church 'devoted themselves to the apostle's teaching?' Are you saying that we should ignore something that the early church obviously did regularly?" This is precisely where it is possible to adhere to something we think is biblical, but in the process refuse to work with the soil God has given us to till, sow, and harvest. This soil requires us to think differently about learning, perhaps in ways that rival the challenges faced after the Gutenberg Press was invented. Maybe what is needed are less teaching experts and more people gifted in the ability to help point others to the right resources at the right time. All of this directly relates to how people are formed as apprentices of Jesus and the kind of environment where apprenticeship might thrive, or be suppressed. But before that environment can be discussed, there is one more sacred cow to kill.

Beyond The Meeting

Bring up the subject of Christianity or church and quickly the discussion will turn to what occurs during the hour or so every Sunday morning in countless church buildings across America. Church is synonymous with the activities of corporate worship and preaching when everyone is dressed in their Sunday best and the pastor is *preaching the Word*. However, when those activities are stripped away or radically modified, you are left with the most nagging question of all, and the essence of our concerns related to apprenticeship: How am I going to live this out in my real life? What does Paul *really* mean by "...offer your bodies as living sacrifices, holy and pleasing to God—this is your spiritual act of worship" (Romans 12.1)?

I think Paul's challenge was to harmonize any

barrier the early Christians had placed between what they considered *sacred* and *secular*. Culture is constantly seeking to segregate our activities and divide our attention towards the kingdom of God. Eugene Peterson's paraphrase embellishes this thought:

> So here's what I want you to do, God helping you: Take your everyday, ordinary life--your sleeping, eating, going-to-work, and walking-around life--and place it before God as an offering. Embracing what God does for you is the best thing you can do for him. Don't become so well-adjusted to your culture that you fit into it without even thinking. Instead, fix your attention on God. You'll be changed from the inside out. (Romans 12.1–2 *The Message*)

Early in our life together, our faith community determined that we would attempt to discover worship within our *sleeping, eating, going-to-work, and walking-around life*. We continued to gather weekly, ate together in the early evening, and then hung around talking until one or two in the morning. In the midst of what looked casual and ordinary on the surface, the Spirit was plumbing the depths of our souls. We were becoming aware that Jesus was always teaching us, even in the most insignificant aspects of our lives. It is precisely in the insignificant where much of life is lived and we either give God access to those parts or attempt to muddle through on our own.

My wife and I adopted a catch phrase we often tell people who inquire about our church: *"It's not about the meeting."* This is frustrating to people who are just looking for a new church service, but I cannot be apologetic. People will put up with all kinds of theological weirdness from churches, but watch out if you ever mess with their symbols.[2] The Jewish people in first century Palestine defined themselves

What Is Church?

by Torah, Temple, Sabbath, Land, and Family. N.T. Wright argues that Jesus' words and actions usurped these major Jewish symbols and offered a Kingdom alternative centered on himself, which of course led to his death on the cross.

Evangelical Christians have generally defined themselves by the symbol of the corporate church gathering. Consider these familiar statements: "I go to such-and-such church on Sunday…I'm a member at First Church of My–town…Yeah, I'm a Christian, I went to my Bible study just last night." This symbol has become just as strong in the minds of many Christians as going to the temple was to a Jew. However, going to a meeting where Christians are present no more makes you a Christian than going to the temple made you Jewish. Although this may seem obvious to most (especially pastors, who seem to have a very difficult time seeing things from their congregation's perspective), it is nonetheless a major stumbling block. Our response should not simply be more meetings or programs. The symbol of *Sunday-go-to-meeting* Christianity will not die easily. Action is required, symbolic action. Something that gets to the root of who we are and who we were meant to be.

Discovering the Essence of Church

There are many people who see what we have seen within the church and immediately proclaim the way to fix things: "We need to be more biblical, to get back to how the first century church did things. If only all these churches would sell off their buildings and start meeting in homes, everything would be different. Shared leadership is the answer. Pastors need to step down and let their flock have a say for once. Theology is too stagnant. We need some fresh ideas about God to stir the pot." And on and on. A few years ago, I stumbled on a group of people who have consistently refused to be satisfied with quick fixes.

What Is Church?

In the early 1950s, there was a simple, unknown Virginian helping to prophetically birth a church fifty years ahead of its time. You have probably never heard of him. Gordon Cosby was the son of a Baptist father and Presbyterian mother who grew up in Depression Era America. During WWII, Gordon became an Army Chaplain and had experiences that changed his life as a Christian, Pastor, and member of the body of Christ. When he returned from the war, he and a small band of seekers began to experiment with what it means to be *the church* in Washington D.C. In 2001, and then again in 2005, I had the privilege of visiting the result of his life's work and investigate the phenomenon that is the Church of the Savior.

Actually, Church of the Savior (COS) no longer exists as an organizational entity. About ten or fifteen years ago, they recognized that the groups that had been birthed from the church's original core really constituted the *essence* of COS. Therefore, there was no need to prop up another structure for simply nostalgic reasons. They just let it die. Now all that exists are unique *mission groups* that each minister to a specific need critical to the underprivileged residents of the Adams Morgan neighborhood in D.C. Within each of these groups is the genetic code that Gordon and his friends have been working out for the past fifty years. This code is really very simple. It is not a church structure, a church growth technique, or special model for *doing church right*, but really a set of deeply held values and commitments.

I had never heard of Gordon Cosby or COS before Todd Hunter mentioned them to me during one of our conversations. It was actually in the context of a discussion we were having on helping people in church find their calling, which usually is associated with a calling into full-time ministry. If you had a call on your life, you were going to be a preacher or a missionary. Nowadays in evangelical circles, calling into ministry can mean becoming part of a large church staff doing a myriad of different jobs. But mostly call has been associated with a career in professional ministry. Todd and I were discussing the possibility that God calls each of us uniquely into a ministry that may for some be very much outside the church world. Someone may be called to the engineering profession or to be a stay-at-home mom. Others may be called to become entrepreneurs and create businesses that bring justice and healing to the underprivileged in our society. Or some of us may just be called to spend a lot of our time interceding on behalf of those who have not yet tasted of God's grace and love in our communities. Are not these functions as important to God as one who commits their life to be a full-time church leader?

COS takes calling very seriously. One of their deep values is to be committed to the process of call. I say process, because we can never fully rest in one particular calling. God is always speaking to us, beckoning us to hear his voice and do what he says. What COS has ingrained into their corporate identity is a long-lasting patience with God's timing. God's ways take time, and you don't always see results in the ways you would expect. A calling never ends up looking like what you thought.

But even before COS dealt with the issue of calling, they asked a very simple, profound, question—"What is church?" Gordon Cosby posed the question another way to us during our first meeting, "What did Jesus intend his church to look like?" Or, "What is the essence of the church?" Now the intent of this question is not to recapture the church in the Book of Acts or to solve all the problems I addressed above. No, the question is, what did Jesus envision his church to look like *in this time and in this place?* What is important to him, now? After all, he is the head of the church, and he thought up the idea of gathering a group of disciples for mutual support in *the Way*. So what was he really after then and what is he after now?

As with calling, I think it's important to realize that we can never fully rest in one definition of church. The question has many different answers for many varied places and times. As a matter of fact, during our first meeting, Cosby offered this word of advice to us young church planters: "Your job is to keep asking that question as long as you live." Because—and this is critical—"We grow by asking the right questions not by getting answers."

Growth in discipleship to Jesus, as in anything worth our effort, requires discipline. He qualified this part of the discussion because people always have a hard time with the word discipline. It is difficult because it conflicts with our freedom. But in fact, as Richard Foster and others have shown, true freedom is really found in discipline. He quoted Dietrich Bonhoeffer in *The Cost of Discipleship*, "When Christ calls a man, he bids him come and die." The purpose of the spiritual disciplines is to open ourselves in an orderly way to God's grace. That means a long, slow, painful death to every flesh way we know. So what do these disciplines look like to a faith community? He suggested a few guidelines. First, they must apply to life. An example of this is the Sabbath rest and recapturing that as part of the way we live. Not in a legalistic way, of course, but as a discipline to open ourselves to rest and grace. Secondly, we need disciplines that deepen the community and create intimacy. Our society fears closeness, so we need to have time to spare in our gatherings so this closeness is fostered. Finally, we need to be with the poor.

When I visited COS for the first time, I was already aware of my lack of concern for the poor. But Cosby threw me a curve ball. To be with the poor is not the same as trying to help the poor. To be with means you are actually trying to understand someone who is not like you. You are developing relationship. This is a much deeper discipline than just meeting what you think their needs are.

While in Washington D.C., I visited two of the mission groups started under the COS umbrella. The first was their housing project called Jubilee Housing. This program was started more than thirty years ago when they purchased an existing apartment building from a slumlord. Totally funded by private donations, they now have over 200 low-income apartments in multiple buildings. The purpose of the buildings is to provide low-cost, clean housing to neighborhood folks who would normally live in slum conditions (or be homeless). Sister organizations, Jubilee Jobs and Columbia Road Health Care, provide the obvious practical means for quality of life improvement. The second ministry we visited was called Samaritan Inns. It was created to get addicts off the streets and provide an avenue towards total life transformation. Incredibly, ninety-six percent of addicts that begin in their twenty-eight-day Alcoholics Anonymous-style program and continue to live in their long-term housing for another two years, stay off drugs. And not only that, but they get jobs, find permanent housing, and many get reunited with lost family members.

Now, if you have been a good evangelical like me, you are probably wondering, "When do these people get saved?" Or, specific to the argument I have been making, "What about discipleship to Jesus—how is this accomplished?"

This was one of the biggest lessons that COS taught me. Here is a group of people that are deeply *Christian*—sold out to our mission to make disciples as Jesus commanded us to. But they have been committed to one poor neighborhood in DC for fifty years. That commitment has led them to make deep sacrifices of time, energy, and money—all outside of what evangelicals would traditionally classify as *church*. For me, this point was driven home when someone from COS was posed a question about how they deal with having to hire professional social workers to provide some support to their ministries. Obviously, not all of them are totally committed to the original values of the church. The response was that they try not to hire outside unless it is absolutely necessary. She quoted Cosby as saying, "I would much rather have someone working in a mission group who is called than one who is qualified." Immediately I remembered sitting around in church meetings saying those same words about worship leaders and nursery workers! What a box-breaker! These people came to the same conclusions about calling, but relating to life and death issues—dealing with people that Jesus loves dearly, but happen to have no home, no money, and a wrecked life. Up until that point, my concerns were making sure someone was there to watch the three year olds during the Sunday service and the worship team's guitars were in tune.

So what does all this mean? I still do not have *a heart for the poor*. Maybe the truth is that no one does. But Jesus does and we are saying that we will go where he leads us. One of the catch phrases around COS is that we have a journey inwards and a journey outwards. Our calling to the poor (or whatever calling we receive to minister the kingdom of God) comes from Jesus—along the inward road. This is what we must begin seeking in earnest. In the midst of that quest as a learning community, to discover the kingdom of God in us and among us, we may just stumble upon the essence of church.

Towards a Learning Community

Early on in the life of our community I made the decision to become a sofa preacher. What does that mean?

What Is Church?

It is that the primary context I use to talk about God's kingdom, the Scriptures, or what it means to follow Jesus is on the sofa or around a dinner table. This means I have sacrificed pulpit preaching in favor of creating spaces for conversation. My friend T is an excellent sofa preacher. In fact, I know of several good ones in our church alone, my wife included. I would even dare to say that if you were to rank the sofa preachers in our church, I would be somewhere in the middle of the pack.

But sofa preaching is really just the tip of the iceberg. In order to create an environment where apprenticeship to Jesus is possible, where people can discover who they were meant to be, and foster a community that represents the rule and reign of God to the world, a radical reorientation is necessary. This involves redefining everything from leadership, to how we care for our children's spiritual nourishment, to how we should respond to a society that ignores the poor. Quick fixes are not an option.

After visiting COS for the first time and then during our first year as a faith community, I quickly became frustrated. There were simply no good models out there to follow anymore. The questions we were asking, and their inherent implications, put us in a position of not having many advocates or friends. I began looking for other examples outside the church of groups or movements that helped shape the environment I was looking for. The first came from an unlikely source—a lifeguard.

A. A. and the Church

Ahren is a lifeguard for the Palm Beach County parks department. One day while our group was worshipping at a beach pavilion, this tall lanky fellow walked up and asked, "Hey, are you guys Christians?" When we first met Ahren, he was fairly certain that we were a bunch of wackos and we were fairly certain he was as well. Perhaps, that is what has sustained our friendship over the years (that was a joke, Ahren).

Ahren is an adult child of an alcoholic and has found great healing and recovery through Al-Anon.[3] He found Jesus through the program, and had recently begun to look for a church to be with other Christians when he found us. Ahren discovered very quickly that church was nothing like Al-Anon or any other twelve-step based group. For one thing, in church you did a lot of sitting and listening. One of the most helpful attributes of twelve-step groups is that you can find healing through hearing other people's stories. Also, it appeared to Ahren that the pastor was far too dominating in the churches he was attending. He was used to an environment where the group had multiple facilitators and the older attendees were given a chance to share their wisdom. Finally, he was confused why churches had to talk about money and giving all the time. Surely, the healing and growth he found in Al-Anon, which cost almost nothing to run, could be duplicated in the church.

These and other issues made it very difficult for Ahren to feel at home in the church. Granted, his approach early on was typically to go up to the pastor after the service and tell him all of these concerns, as if he would find a sympathetic ear. That approach was perhaps an honest attempt to test the waters for change, which was usually met with mouths agape or cold stares. Ahren peppered our group and me with many of the same questions. I know that I frustrated him back then, because my reaction was typically to take in what I was hearing or simply to offer the response, "Man, I don't know, but that is what this group is about. Let's figure out this stuff together." Over time, I became good friends with Ahren and began to learn more about his story. In the process, I began to learn more about the phenomenon of Alcoholics Anonymous (A.A.) and its sister groups.

Even before meeting Ahren, I had been aware that the classic twelve steps of A.A. were a good model for someone who desired to move beyond the addictions of this world to placing full reliance on Jesus. Earlier in Chapter Two, I mentioned a book by Don Williams entitled *Jesus and Addiction*. In this book, Williams shows how many of our relationships in church and our activities as church leaders are codependent and dysfunctional. The twelve steps, which are based on Jesus' teachings from the Sermon on the Mount, offer a simple way to reorient our lives around Jesus and break the cycle of addiction to these things. There have been many other books and programs specifically designed to help disciples of Jesus that utilize the twelve steps. In our community, there have been several people who have gone through them as a means of either breaking addictions or simply to center themselves on the Master. However, in my conversations with Ahren, it was not the twelve steps that caused him so much difficulty in relationship to the church.

Each Group Has But One Primary Purpose...

In 1946, one of the founders of A.A., Bill W, presented "Twelve Suggested Points of A.A. Tradition" in a group newsletter. A.A. had been in existence for only seven years and had grown from 100 to 24,000 members in that time. One of the many challenges A.A. faced dealt with human beings' natural tendency towards desiring recognition and power when an explosion of growth occurs. Bill W. and other people within A.A. determined that instead of fighting this tendency with their own power grab, they would suggest an alternative way—a way that would defuse the power struggle once and for all. The Twelve Traditions were discerned through seeing what *worked* and what *failed* among the many twelve-step groups that were popping up all over the country. In the mind of someone who has found life through a twelve-step group, the traditions and the steps go hand in hand.

For my friend Ahren, early in his journey as a follower of Jesus, he came to the conclusion that church would look very different if it followed the traditions. In fact, the closer he looked at the scriptures and observed the problems inherent in most churches, he wondered if God was leading him to start a small fellowship with this in mind. As Ahren and I discussed this possibility, I began to study the twelve traditions for myself. What I uncovered was a wonderful example of a recent movement that created an environment where becoming an apprentice of Jesus was a natural process. Here are the twelve traditions, in their short form:

The Twelve Traditions of Alcoholics Anonymous

1. Our common welfare should come first; personal recovery depends upon A.A. unity.
2. For our group purpose there is but one ultimate authority—a loving God as He may express Himself in our group conscience. Our leaders are but trusted servants; they do not govern.
3. The only requirement for A.A. membership is a desire to stop drinking.
4. Each group should be autonomous except in matters affecting other groups or A.A. as a whole.
5. Each group has but one primary purpose—to carry its message to the alcoholic who still suffers.
6. An A.A. group ought never endorse, finance, or lend the

A.A. name to any related facility or outside enterprise, lest problems of money, property and prestige divert us from our primary purpose.

7. Every A.A. group ought to be fully self-supporting, declining outside contributions.
8. Alcoholics Anonymous should remain forever nonprofessional, but our service centers may employ special workers.
9. A.A., as such, ought never be organized; but we may create service boards or committees directly responsible to those they serve.
10. Alcoholics Anonymous has no opinion on outside issues; hence the A.A. name ought never be drawn into public controversy.
11. Our public relations policy is based on attraction rather than promotion; we need always maintain personal anonymity at the level of press, radio, and films.
12. Anonymity is the spiritual foundation of all our traditions, ever reminding us to place principles before personalities.

To fully discuss the potential implications of the twelve traditions on church life, I would need to write another book. However, for the purposes of this chapter, I will begin by showing how the traditions help to create an environment where apprenticeship to Jesus is possible.

The first tradition speaks volumes about how this environment is created. Disunity, infighting, power struggles, controversy—this all makes recovery, or in this case *discipleship*, extremely difficult. The church should be an environment of peace, where human beings can catch a glimpse of the eternal kind of life now. This cannot happen if we are constantly bickering about how the church down the street is doing things wrong, or if we ourselves cannot live together in peace.

What Is Church?

Tradition two directs us to place Jesus and his Spirit at the center of any authority structure. Todd Hunter has posed a great question related to this: "How do we lead a group of people who are supposed to be following *Someone else?*" In other words, if the Holy Spirit is truly at the helm of the church, what is the role of leadership? In A.A., leaders fill the role of *trusted servants*. They are the elders who have been through the fires of recovery for many years. However, they do not think of themselves as arrived, for they are still human beings and still alcoholics. It is with this kind of humility that servant leadership should be expressed in the church.

Tradition three maintains that membership in A.A. groups is voluntary. This is certainly true for most churches, and if anything, membership should mean more. However, the simplicity of this tradition is that behind voluntary membership is the reality that without A.A., many of these people would be dead. A church with this environment operates with open hands and arms, but as a person draws closer to Jesus and his or her fellow apprentices, quitting becomes much more of a serious matter.

Tradition four encourages group autonomy in regards to other groups. Of course, this has enormous implications for things like denominations and associations. Many churches already operate autonomously within their denominations, with mixed results. In regards to the question at hand, autonomy deals more with the ability to shape a unique ethos for the people and context in which the group forms. I will discuss this more in Chapter Eight.

Tradition five is critical to creating a healthy environment for apprentices of Jesus. In the book of 1 Corinthians, Paul writes these harrowing words:

> By the grace God has given me, I laid a foundation as
> an expert builder, and someone else is building on it.

But each one should be careful how he builds. For no one can lay any foundation other than the one already laid, which is Jesus Christ. If any man builds on this foundation using gold, silver, costly stones, wood, hay or straw, his work will be shown for what it is, because the Day will bring it to light. It will be revealed with fire, and the fire will test the quality of each man's work. If what he has built survives, he will receive his reward. If it is burned up, he will suffer loss; he himself will be saved, but only as one escaping through the flames. (1 Corinthians 3.10–15)

How easy (and typical) is it for churches to become distracted from our foundation, and singular primary purpose, which is Christ himself and the Good News of his kingdom. Living out that primary purpose is not easy. However, if we are distracted or place our focus elsewhere, apprenticeship to the Master becomes a distant reality.

Traditions six through nine deal with A.A.'s relationship to infrastructure, staff, and organization. This is essentially where, according to recent statistics, approximately seventy percent of the forty billion or so that is donated to churches annually in the United States goes to maintain. Tradition six states the problem succinctly: "…lest problems of money, property, and prestige divert us from our primary purpose."

Tradition ten again encourages commitment to the primary purpose by keeping A.A. out of the public eye. Imagine for a second (if this is even possible) if the church had never created the *Moral Majority* or if in popular opinion being an evangelical equals being a right-wing Republican. Instead, imagine that followers of Jesus had simply stuck to their objective, to "train everyone you meet, far and near, in this way of life," how things might be different.

This leads to tradition eleven, which supports the

idea that the best marketing tool for A.A. is the people themselves and their individual stories. Why promote something through expensive advertising when alcoholics are attracted to the program through the healing stories of their friends? Does it not say something about the quality of discipleship lived within churches that spend millions of dollars on advertising? This is certainly a controversial argument, yet A.A. stands as a living witness to the power of story as a means of inviting people into the kingdom of God.

The final tradition, which is the heart of the *anonymous* part of A.A., is an uncomfortable reminder of the lengths we have gone to ignore some of the plainest teachings of the New Testament. Paul says, again in 1 Corinthians, "One of you says, 'I follow Paul'; another, 'I follow Apollos'; another, 'I follow Cephas'; still another, 'I follow Christ.' Is Christ divided? Was Paul crucified for you? Were you baptized into the name of Paul?" (1 Corinthians 1.12–13) And then later in Chapter 2,

> When I came to you, brothers, I did not come with
> eloquence or superior wisdom as I proclaimed to you
> the testimony about God. For I resolved to know
> nothing while I was with you except Jesus Christ
> and him crucified. I came to you in weakness and
> fear, and with much trembling. My message and my
> preaching were not with wise and persuasive words,
> but with a demonstration of the Spirit's power, so
> that your faith might not rest on men's wisdom, but
> on God's power. (1 Corinthians 2.1–5)

Apprentices of Jesus are nothing in ourselves. We are, as Paul, simply heralds of the King, servants and friends to those who are lost and without hope. This is the stunning reality that A.A. has represented so well and the church often fails at so miserably. We are more interested in making a name for ourselves, or our church, than in following the narrow path that leads to life.

There could be more to say about A.A. and how it relates to the church in our time, but I believe a fairly clear image has been presented of what might be possible. A.A. represents how small gatherings of Jesus' apprentices, with no resources and a minimum amount of training and organization, can turn the world upside down. In our community, we have not wholesale adopted the traditions as our own, but they inform many of our common practices and thinking. We are attempting to learn from their example and continue pressing forward as a family of disciples.

Free Play in God's Kingdom

The final element to creating an environment where apprenticeship to Jesus is possible comes from even a more unlikely source than A.A.: early childhood education. In the early 1900s, Maria Montessori, a physician and professor of anthropology at the University of Rome, challenged the dominant theories about how children learn. Her research, which mostly occurred among the orphans and physically and mentally handicapped children of the city's asylums, demonstrated that children are not born with *ready-made* brains. "For all the previous centuries, educators had deemed the child an essentially formed being and thus a vehicle ready to receive knowledge previously discovered and digested by others."[4] Montessori actually discovered the complete opposite was true. The human brain needed an environment early in life where it could be trained to self-develop. She saw that children under six absorb tremendous amounts of information from their environment, through use of each of their five senses. However, she also observed that children did not show interest in particular areas of learning equally or simultaneously. Their interest in one activity might grow to a peak for a period of time and then be transferred to a completely different activity for another period of time. Recognition of these *sensitive periods* as she called them helped her craft an environment where individual children had the freedom to be focused on the area of development that mattered to them most.

Some educators have criticized this model as a free-for-all that encourages lack of discipline in a child. However, what Montessori concluded was that during this stage of life—particularly age three to six—a child's natural self-preoccupation provided the energy and focus for them to self-develop. Any parent has observed their three year old find *work*, whether it be washing pretend dishes or digging in the flower beds, and stay focused on this task for long periods of time. Montessori simply translated that reality into a learning environment where children are able to maximize their self-development opportunities through each sensitive period.

After age six, Montessori observed that children became much more socially aware, becoming *social explorers* rather than *sensorial explorers*. As a result, the learning environment after six changes into one geared towards social development and learning within groups. During this stage, Montessori observed,

> ...an intense absorption with issues of good and evil, justice and injustice, loyalty and disloyalty, and the rules and rituals of the group. The child has extraordinary energy and is physically healthier than in the earlier period. With his immediate curiosity about all of life and his newly formed powers of reason, the child at this stage is in his most intense period of learning.[5]

What Is Church?

The stages from age twelve to eighteen, and eighteen to twenty-four mirror the first two stages of development, resulting in a fully-formed adult.

Two of my children have had the opportunity to learn in a Montessori environment. Sadly, due to the cost of the manipulatives and compensation required for qualified teachers, Montessori schools can be quite expensive. However, the principles are transferable even for parents who teach at home or whose children are in the public school system. Sofia Cavalletti developed an early childhood catechesis based on Montessori's research and her own observations on the spiritual formation of children. What is fascinating about her work and the curriculum she developed, "The Catechesis of the Good Shepherd," is that it is not difficult to extrapolate into formation of the church as a whole. In the Foreword to her book, *The Religious Potential of the Child*, it is written of her:

> Cavalletti is never distracted by her own agenda from the real goal of the Christian life: to live a life hidden with God in Christ. Too often religious education is so goal-oriented and curriculum-conscious that it loses sight of its mission to minister to the religious life of the child. Adult education likewise easily degenerates into indoctrination or dissolves into vapid 'sharing'... This never happens with Cavalletti...It is important to recognize that she does not discourse at length about the religious experience of children. It is a mystery to be respected. All she will do, is report on what we might call the 'symptoms' of that mystery: the sense of engagement, the quiet joy, the recognition of the truth of biblical or liturgical presentation, and the short, sharp insights offered spontaneously by children that, together with their drawings, represent the fruits of their contemplation of the mystery. This is what the

catechesis is about. Is it not what all ministry is about: encounter with the mystery of God?[6]

I wish to use the example of Montessori and Cavalletti to confront some of our arrogance regarding spiritual formation. Typical church learning structures model seminaries because that is all we know. But injecting an average young Christian into that environment is the spiritual equivalent of enrolling your five year old in a freshman level Chemistry class, expecting him to explain the periodic chart, then walk down the street to the corner drug store and begin working as a pharmacist. The converse is true as well. Our structures are such that we take people who could be ministering at a high level, mature Christians with years of life experience, and dump them in the lobby handing out bulletins or teaching a small group on rehashed notes from last week's sermon.

Apprenticeship to Jesus might be more of a reality, if the context for learning was more conducive to the way individuals actually learn. As a young Christian, just as a young child, there are sensitive periods of growth that we experience. We are enlightened by the scriptures in new ways and confronted with our sin and disease of self-worship. We fumble our way through these new discoveries and attempt to process what it means to be a part of the family of God. The earliest Christians appeared to have radically different ideas about what these first years of a disciple should look like:

> It is quite clear that the Early Church, which prescribed that potential disciples be trained for three years, was in no hurry to pack their congregations full of warm bodies. Rather, understanding patience as one of the primary characteristics of God's nature, and remembering the Apostle Paul's teaching that

the love to which we are called is first of all patient
(1 Cor. 13.4), they sought to guide catechumens
toward repentance, a turning from the powers of the
world that ensnared them. It was not enough for a
person to commit their bodies to participating in
the worship of the Church, but rather the complete
person was to be submitted to the work of God. And
if a person encountered obstacles that interfered with
the Holy Spirit's transforming work, the Church was
to bear patiently with that person for whatever length
of time it took until he or she was set free from major
patterns of sin and ready for baptism.[7]

This kind of transformation simply cannot happen
in an eight week *New Believers* class, no matter how good
the teaching or content. As the Family of God, we look at
new apprentices as adopted children, just as we were once
adopted into Christ's fold. Just as parents who adopt must
struggle to help the child adjust to a new family with a
different relational dynamic, so must we do the same for
new Christians.

Beyond the first few years, there is a slow redirection
that occurs to identifying with God's action in the world.
It is at this point, that a true, living and breathing learning
community is possible. Free play in God's kingdom becomes
a reality. Working together: from birth to death, being
trained, and training others in the glory of God and his way
of life. This is possible if we are able to let go of our current
models of dominance, where the *big jug* is constantly seeking
to fill the *little mugs* with the right answers, or the right
actions. In a learning community, leadership gifts finally find
their true home as that which becomes the servant of all.

The role of the minister, then, must be self-effacing…
in terms of not needing to be in control, and more

specifically of not needing to count the fruits of one's labors. What counts is not whether we get the results we want but whether the faithful are able to drink of the living streams.[8]

Treasure Hunters

Hopefully, I have been able to demonstrate how it is possible for a small group of people to create an environment where apprenticeship to Jesus is a natural outcome, or at least not neglected or discouraged. There is no magic formula for creating this environment, however. Our process in South Florida will no doubt look much different in other parts of the country or world. The one common denominator will be the leadership of Jesus and the process of each of us becoming more like him.

Towards the end of Willard's book *Renovation of the Heart*, he describes the tension that churches face between what they think of as normal church activities and apprenticeship to Jesus.[9] Why are we so distracted from the simple and primary goal of Christlikeness? Maybe it is because we have spent so much time focusing on the *vessel* of church rather than the *treasure* of Jesus and his ways. In 2 Corinthians 4.6-7, Paul uses this analogy to describe how in the weakness of his body, God is glorified because it is his power that is making us new: "But we have this treasure in earthen vessels, that the surpassing greatness of the power may be of God and not from ourselves." The same could be said of our churches, denominations, and other ministry organizations. These vessels are broken, imperfect bodies, destined for death. Like our own human bodies, we spend so much time primping and preening, obsessed with elements that are one day going to return to dust. As the saying goes, "You can't make a silk purse out of a sow's ear." In this case, if we mistake the vessel of church for the treasure of Jesus, we cannot assume anything beautiful or *godly* will come out of it.

So what are these *vessel matters* we should avoid? A helpful question to ask might be, "Am I more concerned about getting this part of church right instead of becoming right myself?" Vessels do not transform us, but they can take us to places where we can be transformed. If I knew that a wealthy person across town was going to give me a new car if I found a way to get to his house, I would not complain that I had to ride a smelly, crowded bus to get there. Jesus is offering us a radically transformed life, culminating in the greatest gift of all—resurrection, new life for eternity. Constantly griping about the transportation he has provided is kind of shallow compared to that gift, don't you think?

But some are probably protesting at this point, "Haven't you spent this entire book griping about the vessel? Isn't this book a polemic against *church as we've known it*? Aren't you just wasting your time?" I think if you look carefully, you will see that the questions I have been raising in this book and been wrestling with for the past few years are because I want to see more of God's treasure. We have been so obsessed with the smelly, crowded bus we are riding on that we have forgotten where it is going. These questions, this whole confusing and often painful journey is all about waking up to where Jesus is leading us. It is about stripping down the vessel to the point where it does not require constant maintenance. We are treasure hunters. Our transportation is important, but we don't spend a lot of time fussing over it. We use it, tweak it if necessary, and tow it to the junkyard when it breaks down on the side of the road.

One of the beautiful things about becoming a treasure hunter is meeting others with the same passion. When the vessel becomes something secondary, it creates space to look around, to see how others are being apprenticed to the Master. Within the church, there is an underground movement of these apprentices who are slowly finding each other—the Jesus Underground.

Chapter Seven
The Jesus Underground

In Christendom, we are primarily identified with the name
of the church, denomination, or organization of which
we are affiliated: Baptist, Presbyterian, Church of Christ,
Saddleback Church, Willow Creek, Campus Crusade,
Compassion International. However, many Christians are
mutts when it comes to their spiritual heritage. For example,
my family went from Lutheran to independent charismatic
to Calvary Chapel during my childhood. I then was involved
in Campus Crusade for Christ at the University of Florida,
a Baptist church and an Evangelical Free church for a while,
then finally a Vineyard church. Brian McLaren wrote a
book a few years ago with the (sort-of) tongue-in-cheek
title, *A Generous Orthodoxy: Why I Am a Missional, Evangelical,
Post/Protestant, Liberal/Conservative, Mystical/Poetic, Biblical,*

What Is Church?

Charismatic/Contemplative, Fundamentalist/Calvinist, Anabaptist/Anglican, Methodist, Catholic, Green, Incarnational, Depressed-yet-Hopeful, Emergent, Unfinished CHRISTIAN. The ironic thing, of course, is that McLaren's name is thought to be synonymous with Emergent than it is with any of those other categories.

Once a Christian settles on a particular tribe, especially as a pastor or church leader, it is often easy to dismiss or belittle the experiences had before in other denominations or churches. The result is most typically a kind of tribalism that envisions the denomination or movement as synonymous with one's spiritual family. For a pastor in that context, climbing the corporate ladder within the family's hierarchy becomes an assumed goal. A self-sustaining church, the normal rhythm of board meetings and event planning, preaching, counseling, attending pastor's meetings, going on a missions trip once in awhile. This is the American Pastoral Dream. Add to that some recognition within the family that you are a success by giving you an overseer position or a place on the national board of directors and you reached the pinnacle.

It should be obvious by now that the American Pastoral Dream was lost on me quite a while ago. However, the Dream did not die quickly or easily. In fact, even in the midst of the rethinking of my role that I described in Chapter Three, I still imagined that one day I would be received among my tribe as someone who took an alternative path, but held true to basic values that held us together. In my mind, the possibility existed that even though I had a full-time engineering job and was not pursuing the expected career path as a full-time minister, that I would be recognized for the journey we had embarked on and dream we had pursued. Perhaps I was just young and presumptuous. Perhaps I cared too much about what others thought about me. Whatever the reasons, my experience involved going through the pain of losing a family, but uncovering one whose diversity and size has the potential of bringing much change to the world.

Drifting Away

The Well began as a church plant of the Vineyard Christian Fellowship of Gainesville, Florida. The Vineyard was my tribe from about 1994 and I was ordained by the church in Gainesville in 2001. The process of leaving Gainesville was a difficult one as we were not only moving to a new town, but would be leaving a family. The pastor, Arty Hart, and his wife Jackie had been dear friends and mentors to us. There were many others from the church who had a profound impact on us as we prepared for this new work. We also had greatly benefited from the wider Vineyard movement in our training and preparation. As I mentioned in an earlier chapter, I am a graduate of Vineyard Leadership Institute in Columbus, Ohio. We attended multiple Vineyard leadership conferences and church planting workshops. We also learned the art of leading worship from some of the best songwriters and worship leaders in the country. Finally, through the ministry of John Wimber and from years of practical experience in Gainesville, we received countless lessons about the ministry of the Holy Spirit. We saw and participated in healings, deliverance from demonization, and prophetic ministry. In the space of about five years, our ministry tools were sharpened and used to great effect. This was invaluable experience that we carried with us to South Florida. As Vineyard church planters, we were well prepared.

For the first few years of our journey, we continued the best we could to stay connected to the Vineyard and

What Is Church?

our church family in Gainesville. However, this increasingly became difficult when I made the decision to work as an engineer again. Pastor's meetings just are not designed for people who work normal forty-hour-a-week jobs. Also, I began to recognize that our experiences as a church were not always the easiest to explain to my Vineyard brothers and sisters. For example, because our gatherings were in homes, there were several pastors who assumed I was associated with the House Church movement. I explained that we only met in homes out of convenience and cost, but it was a difficult sell. For many of the pastors, we were simply rehashing questions they had (and lessons they learned) in the 1970s during the Jesus movement. Imagine taking a vacation day from work to travel to a leadership meeting in order to maintain relationships with people who mostly misunderstood everything that came out of your mouth. Frustrating at best.

Regardless, we had no intention of leaving the Vineyard movement or purposefully damaging any of our relationships with the Vineyard family. However, soon I found myself having an incredibly difficult phone conversation with my overseer. It is not important what was said during that conversation or what precipitated it in the first place. The outcome was clear—we needed to seriously think about our relationship to the Vineyard movement. Was it something our community needed? Was it helpful for Amber and me to continue trying to make ourselves understood and to work to build bridges?

We sought the council of some trusted friends, mentors, and our community. Vineyard friends from other parts of the country found it difficult to relate to our predicament. Early on, I was convinced that we would continue to try and make the relationship work, in spite of the challenges. I did not like the idea of leaving a family that had given me so much and to which I had invested so much for over ten years. However, our primary concern was caring for our church family in South Florida and allowing the Holy Spirit to lead us to whatever would be most helpful to what he was doing there. After much prayer and discussion, we decided corporately to leave the Vineyard in March 2006.

Some may be wondering why I decided to write about this part of our story. It may have been easier, and perhaps more generous, to simply omit it altogether and just talk about the future of local and trans-local relationships within the church. As difficult as it is to write about, I believe it would be a disservice to others to not tell the story. Many on this journey have gone through hell trying to reconcile relationships with their spiritual families. Others have simply been cast out and forgotten. What we experienced was in some ways like a childhood friendship growing cold. There was no anger or mean-spiritedness. We did not feel betrayed by our brothers and sisters or even feel that the situation was unjust in any way. It was what it was. We drifted apart and there simply was not time or energy on our part (or necessity from our community's point of view) to prop up a dying friendship.

As a reader, you might not agree with our decision. You may even be concerned for our welfare, that we have disassociated ourselves from a system of accountability, wisdom, and history. Yet what we are beginning to uncover— indeed what has been there and is growing every day—is a vast network of people and churches that also have the kingdom of God as their primary concern. These people come from tribes of every stripe. They represent countless varieties of what John Wimber called *God's Big Bride*, the Church. And the relationships being formed among this diversity are advancing a revolution of unity and love that is creating a new foundation for what it means to be a part of a spiritual family.

What Is Church?

The Order of Elpida

In Chapter Four, I told the story of Mark Palmer and Chad Canipe; two friends whose stories paralleled ours in many ways but were tragically cut short. The group of friends I described in that chapter who knew Mark and Chad were born out of a common determination to not be afraid to ask questions like "What is church?" Unlike so many of our peers, our desire to be together was not because we hoped to start the next Great American Church Movement. We simply needed the company. We needed to be around others that did not think we were crazy. We also needed companions that would not drop us if we failed to *produce* from a ministry perspective.

About a year before he died, Mark Palmer challenged us as friends to covenant with one another towards that long-term companionship. On his right forearm, Mark bore a tattoo that held great significance to him. It was of a tree with long branches stretching towards the sky with the word ελπίδα below. Ελπίδα (or *elpida* in English letters) is the Greek word for *hope*. Combined with the tree image, this embodied Mark's anticipation of God's kingdom—both what he is doing now and will do in the future, particularly the resurrection and restoration of all things. This image and word also became significant to our little group of friends. Many of us had come to the stark realization that we had been placing our hope in our stature among other Christian leaders, or in our ability to organize church events, or our theological prowess. With all of that taken away, we were left with really the only hope we had in the first place. Mark cautioned us on the gravity of our decision to covenant together. His cancer was evidence enough that the stakes were high. Would we be willing to walk with him, even through death, with only the stubborn hope that somehow God would eventually turn the world right side up?

What Is Church?

Over the course of this book, I have attempted to provide an apologetic for a way forward in this rapidly morphing church climate. There are options galore for anyone not content to sit on their hands and wait for Jesus to come back. The problem is most of the options include us getting our hands a little too busy too fast. Instead, what if we stood at these crossroads and effectively said, "Maybe the way forward is actually to slow down, to count the cost of discipleship. Maybe the way forward is to die?" But in dying, we open ourselves to possibilities that are not available to the spiritual entrepreneurs of the world. In death, the only possibility is resurrection. Our only shot is God. There is no pulling oneself up by the bootstraps and making a name for yourself when you're dead. There is no organizing yourself out of death. You can cast vision all you want, host conferences, start foundations, propose initiatives. Not when you're dead. "For you died, and your life is now hidden with Christ in God."[74] Your life, your whole life, *your real life*, *is* hidden with Christ in God. That means when someone looks at your life and what you accomplish, they probably won't see you, they'll see Jesus. That is the only way I see forward. Everything else just leaves me having to die all over again.

The Order of Elpida is simply a group of friends who have agreed to die together and put all our hope for a preferable future in the hands of King Jesus. Some of us have small faith communities where we attempt to practice our gifts and callings in ways that are faithful to the Way of Jesus. Some are in more traditional churches laboring for the kingdom there. Others are alone, wrestling with these realities as families with little daily support. But we all share the same desire—to see God's kingdom made more real in the world and to live lives pleasing to Jesus.

Is there a way to reproduce the Order of Elpida? I

don't even know if that is the right question to ask. These relationships were not planned. We had no organizational aspirations and even resisted the idea that we could somehow spark a *movement*. Honestly, these relationships were about our survival more than anything else. We are not influential people in the wider Christian conversation, at least in terms of being recognized authors or known speakers. Collectively, our faith communities do not amount to much on paper. But now five years later, I know I am going to survive. In fact, I have great hope for our future, what God is doing, and how he is going to use us. We don't have all the answers. We aren't qualified to prescribe a step-by-step plan for planting the next great emerging church or creating some world-changing organization. Ours has been a way of waiting, questions, pain, and even death. Not fun stuff. Not *host the next big innovative conference and sell a million books* kind of stuff, that's for sure. But I would rather have a few friends that will call me brother for life than a successful book deal or my name on a conference agenda. For that reason, I believe something incredible is possible for those of us who have died to those aspirations.

The Jesus Underground

Imagine if all Christian resources were suddenly not available. What if travel was restricted so it was impossible to attend a conference or hear a nationally recognized speaker? (This is not a stretch if gas prices rise to eight dollars a gallon or something insane like that.) What if religious organizations could no longer own property? What if the economy was so bad no one had any money to give towards building projects in the first place? Obviously, things would change. The church would adapt. In China, the persecuted church grew by some estimates from seven million to 130

million in less than thirty years, a forty-three-fold increase.[1]
This explosion came through simple gospel sharing, through
relationship, friend to friend, house to house, co-worker to
co-worker. No program and no control. Just people sharing
Jesus.

Is this possible in our time and culture? Should we even
expect this kind of explosive growth? Anything can happen,
but I don't think the Chinese believers in the late 70s sat
back and wondered "What can we do to have a forty-three-
fold increase in the population of Christians in thirty years?"
They simply did what they could with the resources they
had and put their ultimate trust in God's provision. I don't
think we in the West will be experiencing the same kind
of religious persecution anytime soon. However, if we are
honest with ourselves, and the state of lived Christianity in
the West, we will admit that we are facing a crisis that the
best of our spiritual technology just cannot fix.

In Chapter Five, I described how followers of Jesus
might identify with the ways and means of subversives
in order to faithfully express the kingdom of God as a
local community. This is a deeply pastoral task, one that
requires leadership and innovative thinking. However, it
also requires a patient repudiation of ways and means that
disallow the Holy Spirit from taking his rightful place as the
central authority and spiritual director of each individual.
If you have been a leader in the church, I promise you,
this will be the most challenging leadership assignment
you have ever had. Leading in this manner is taxing to the
mind and spirit, and devastating to the ego. The rewards are
small, the thank-yous rare. There are vocational challenges,
as I described in Chapter Three. This community of
subversives will be messy and seemingly out of control at
times, as I described in Chapter Four. Retraining a group
of people whose steady diet of self-help sermons has left

their theological bones weak, their imaginations stifled, and their ability to self-learn undermined will feel like a lost cause. For these reasons and more, you will find yourself longing for allies, not just encouragement you might find from reading a book like this, downloading a podcast, or following someone's blog. You will want someone to tell you face-to-face, "You are not crazy. You are not weird. The path you are on is leading somewhere because the Holy Spirit is leading you. I will go along for the ride with you."

Over the past seven years I have met and befriended other leaders undergoing this transition. Beyond Elpida, there are acquaintances scattered around the country I could count on as allies in a time of need or encouragement. We have dear friends who are missionaries in Arequipa, Peru, that we met through our website and blog. Recently our family spent five weeks on an experimental trip to Peru to support our friends, experience a new culture, and build in some sabbatical time. This was not classic short-term missions, building or evangelizing or teaching the whole time. It was an experiment in cross-pollination: learning together, stretching, growing, sharing our experience and visa-versa. The *results* were a renewed passion for our community, for our calling, and to continue pursuing our place in God's story. We had a great experience as a family, learning how to survive in another culture, and teaching our children a little more about the world. We also were able to reassure a Peruvian pastor, who was forced out of his denomination, and other local believers struggling with the church, with the knowledge that they were part of God's family and we counted them as brothers and sisters. It was small, mustard-seed work. No great revival of the masses. No church-planting initiatives. Just simple people receiving and embodying the beautiful, free, life-giving message of God's kingdom.

It should be stating the obvious by now to say that

there are many people who call themselves followers of Jesus who need this kind of simple encouragement. As American Christians, we have a knee-jerk response to need. We want to host conferences, call round-tables, start revivals, and inevitably start movements. We think that all this activity somehow makes those in need feel *included.* In my experience the opposite is true. All of our efforts do little more than to create a wall of inaccessibly. "You'll never be as smart as that author at the round-table. You'll never speak as well as that pastor at that conference. You'll never be as gifted as that evangelist leading the revival. You'll never be a leader like that person in charge of the movement." If there be any doubt, let me state this in plain language—None of that matters. Being smart at a round-table does not matter. Being able to speak well does not matter. Leading a revival meeting does not matter. Organizational leadership *does not matter.*

Did you hear me? Really?

If you still doubt me, let me rattle off a few names for you:

Joseph. The runt of his family, left for dead in a well, enslaved, held prisoner for no crime…became the savior of one nation and father of another.

Moses. Had the audacity to tell God (who was speaking to him in an audible voice) that he could not speak well enough to lead the people of Israel out of Egypt.

Paul. Laughed at by the so-called smart people of his day.

Peter. Resumé: fisherman, denier of Christ, hot-head, difficult to work with. Father of the church.

The Jesus Underground will be made up of ordinary

citizens of the kingdom Jesus proclaimed and lived. As people are freed from the expectations of those trying to bring the kingdom through their gifting or organization or brains, they will agree with the one who said, "Seek first the kingdom of God and his righteousness, and all these things will be added to you." The Jesus Underground will agree with his ways, his word. They will consider themselves to be of the same family, yet will appreciate their diversity and different callings. They will ask questions together, learn together, grow together, weep together, rejoice together. God will do tremendous things through them, but you most likely will never read their names on a conference program or on the back of a best-selling book. They will never be able to form a movement as they are embedded among all facets of the church and cross every cultural boundary. But in a generation, they will have brought tremendous change to the church and to the world. There will be leadership among these people, but it will take forms unique to the time in which we live. I like to call this leadership Apostle 2.0.

Apostle 2.0. Releasing the Jesus Underground

We typically think of the early apostles as having this happy-go-lucky lifestyle, traveling all over the Mediterranean, preaching, planting churches, healing people, and writing scripture on the side. Paul wakes us up to reality in 1 Corinthians 4:

> For I think that God has exhibited us apostles as last of all, like men sentenced to death, because we have become a spectacle to the world, to angels, and to men. We are fools for Christ's sake, but you are wise in Christ. We are weak, but you are strong. You are held in honor, but we in disrepute. To the present hour we hunger and thirst, we are poorly dressed

and buffeted and homeless, and we labor, working with our own hands. When reviled, we bless; when persecuted, we endure; when slandered, we entreat. We have become, and are still, like the scum of the world, the refuse of all things. (1 Corinthians 4.9–13, English Standard Version)

Wow, that sounds attractive! Sign me up! But yet we still have this glamorous, idealized image of apostleship that distorts an indispensable role necessary for the church's bleeding edge. Instead of abandoning the role, what if it was recast as someone who gives themselves to connect the church, this Jesus Underground, in life-giving ways? We might call such a person a *Wide-Area Networker*.

All of us live in an immense web of interconnected networks that relate on countless levels and through a variety of means. It is still shocking sometimes to think that only a few years ago I was unsure if anyone else was asking questions like "What is church?" The speed and accessibility to people and ideas the internet provides has literally made some of the more formal and traditional means for connection obsolete. If we take seriously what Paul says is one of the aims of an apostle's work, to "attain to the unity of the faith," then the internet is potentially one of the most powerful tools available for encouraging that end. Petty theological arguments aside, those with a mind towards connecting the church for the sake of the kingdom have at their fingertips an incredible advantage over their counterparts ten or fifteen years ago.

Wide-Area Networkers (WANs) function very much like the servers they utilize to transfer emails and data from the web all around the world. They are the servers of the church, creating pathways for people to be in communion with their brothers and sisters who gather in homes or ornate cathedrals and everything in between. In this way, their function is extremely utilitarian relative to the real work of the church—announcing the kingdom in word and deed. They may garner recognition and admiration for their abilities, but in the end they are really not much more than a conduit for relationship, blessing, encouragement, compassion, grace, and love to pass between outposts of God's church. A spectacle indeed.

So who can fill this role? Well, it certainly doesn't require a degree or a full-time salary. However, it does require a willingness to drop some of the traditional ministry aspirations that plague the church's ability to facilitate unity. WANs are not primarily concerned with building their *brand* (i.e. denomination or particular church flavor). Instead, they seek to enable productive interactions between dissimilar segments of the church in order for the focus to be shifted back towards God's purposes and his heart. Typically, WANs have a very simple and singular message. They tell stories—the same stories—over and over and over. But it is these stories that get underneath the skin of sectarian tendencies and draw the church together. Pretty soon, you find Catholics and Baptists sharing notes and trading ideas, Vineyard people and Presbyterians confessing their love for a particular author, or a house church leader and a megachurch youth pastor sharing coffee at their favorite cafe.

One excellent example of a WAN is Andrew Jones. Andrew helped to get many people involved in blogging, but I believe his greater gift has been to model what it might look like to be a connecting node in the wide area network of church, and to culture, in general. His contribution to the emerging church conversation (not simply to the organization called Emergent, but to the conversation regarding how the church transitions in light of a rapidly changing society) is enormous. Reading his blog over the last few years, I have noticed him continually building up those he comes in contact with and spending time encouraging pilgrims and kingdom workers from all over the world. His family has moved too many times to count, but it seems that everywhere they land, they immediately begin ministering locally while continuing to connect globally. There is an inherent playfulness in Andrew's reporting of their life and ministry that seems to come from a deep awareness that he is *not* building God's kingdom, but is simply living in its ebb and flow. That awareness is the key to fruitfulness as a Wide Area Networker.

The Jesus Underground is an uncontrollable, morphing network of people that love Jesus and serve his kingdom vision. People will still start their movements, host their conferences, and lead their revivals. But behind the scenes, the unknowns of the church will be quietly growing in number and influence. They believe the words of their master: "Blessed are the meek, for they shall inherit the earth."

Chapter Eight
Undercovering an Ethos

Jesus...envisaged that, scattered around Palestine, there would be small groups of people loyal to himself, who would get together to encourage one another, and would act as members of a family, sharing some sort of common life and, in particular, exercising mutual forgiveness. It was because this way of life was what it was, while reflecting the theology it did, that Jesus' whole movement was thoroughly, and dangerously, 'political'. And...the main characteristic of the cells that Jesus called into being was of course loyalty to Jesus himself.[1]

After six years, what has asking questions like *"What is church?"* produced in these little unknown groups of people like ours in South Florida? Certainly nothing noteworthy by recent church planting standards. We are still small churches without influence in the larger Christian community. Several of my friends have decided to fold themselves and their communities back into other local churches or have simply dissolved. But there are those of us who are stubborn enough to keep moving forward, often with very few tangible evidences of growth or encouragement. For us, and I will speak now only for our church in Jupiter, some roots are beginning to find their way into deeper soil. This has caused us to recognize that there is a social reality which we live by that was not my idea or something we copied from someone else.

Traditionally, this has boiled down to what churches like to call *values*. Values are generally something that a pastor writes and then posts on the wall in the church lobby for the ushers to read between services. In other words, no one knows what they are, and no one cares. Instead of values, what we have uncovered is something more like an *ethos*. Dictionary. com defines *ethos* as:

> The fundamental character or spirit of a culture; the underlying sentiment that informs the beliefs, customs, or practices of a group or society.[2]

Values are imposed from without, ethos is cultivated within. So in other words, I can neither take the credit or the blame for the ethos that our church has developed. It is simply the way things are, for good or ill, based on a long process that I did not control.

There is something else that needs to be clearly expressed before discussing this ethos. What has developed in our church as a result of this journey of asking questions is by no means prescriptive for the church in general. As I stated earlier, our story is not one of attempting to recapture the first century church or be more biblical than everyone else. It is rather a story of brokenness—people attempting to sort through the lessons of the past and stumble forward into the light of God's kingdom.

The Way of Jesus, Teaching, and Participation

Dallas Willard once asked a great (and terrifying) question:

> When do you suppose was the last time any group of believers or church of any kind or level had a meeting of its officials in which the topic for discussion and action was how they were going to teach their people actually to do the specific things Jesus said?[3]

When the gravity of that question sinks in, you realize that we can no longer just sit around and learn about what Jesus said, or debate his words, or just put them into nice worship songs. The Way of Jesus must be attempted or it is not a Way at all. This is the first aspect of our ethos—we are people of the Way. Conversations on what Jesus really meant when he said, "Do not judge...," and then intentionally practicing that as a course of life are indicative of people that are trying to live the Way of Jesus.

Related to this, of course, is how teaching happens. A three-point message on *not judging* with a handy fill-in-the-blanks bulletin insert is a wonderful Bible stuffer, but in the internet age, acquisition of knowledge is the easy part. You can probably download that insert somewhere without having to sit through a two hour service.

My brother Mark was part of our original faith community. After decompressing from hearing two sermons a week for his entire Christian experience, he made this statement: "I am now aware that my knowledge of the Bible far outweighs my obedience to the Bible." This has become the stark truth for many of us with deep Christian roots.

What Is Church?

For those with less knowledge, experience has shown that much can be learned by simply being around people who are trying to live this stuff. As we sit on the couch together and you tell me of your struggles, the book you are reading, the Scripture you are meditating on, I learn. The best sermons are sometimes the ones when we do not even know anyone is preaching.

That flows into another fairly obvious aspect of this ethos: everybody gets to play.[4] Whether it be in a gathering or going to help someone fix up a rental property, we must practice the reality that we are all free as God's people to serve in whatever capacity the Holy Spirit sees fit. I have a college degree, a ministry degree, years of experience leading small groups, leading worship teams, overseeing all sorts of ministries, counseling, preaching, organizing, doing ministry stuff. Yet it is my unmitigated joy when an eleven-year-old girl raises her hand during a meeting, asks a question theologians have been debating for centuries, and stops all of us so-called *ministers* in our tracks. Everyone gets to play, everyone has a voice, participation over performance.

Blurring the Boundaries, Fitting In, and Sticking it Out Together

A few years ago, it was inferred by an older Christian that I had a *chip on my shoulder* regarding church. Although this criticism stung a little, I spent some time really trying to determine if it was true. The comment came in the midst of a very difficult conversation, one I was quite sure there was little hope that I would be able to adequately explain myself. Eventually, I realized that I did have a *chip* after all, but it was not in regards to church. It was because I felt on several occasions misunderstood, not listened to, and not respected.

What Is Church?

What if a group of people decided that instead of defending their boundaries of who is *in* or *out*, *right* or *wrong*, *leader* or *follower*, that they instead determined to engage each other as human beings, sinners, and children of God? At that starting place, there are several things that happen in that group of people all at once. First of all, it leaves little room for ego to rear its ugly head. Second, judgmentalism in all of its forms takes a backseat to hospitality, freedom, and compassion. Finally, an environment is fostered where *fitting in* has nothing to do with how well you measure up to what the group determines is cool or what might classify you as a misfit.

I am learning to let go of that chip that I described above. However, that process is not something natural or even encouraged in most Christian contexts. If you are *in*, you are taught to root out error, expose heresy, keep the boundaries safe and secure. If you are *out*, you are encouraged to embrace the attitude of an innovator and reject your critics as fundamentalists. The problem in both cases is that it is very easy to lose your soul in the process of figuring out what side of the fence you are on.

As God's family, we must be willing the walk into the fray and figure out how to love people as they are, listen to their stories, and attempt to see how the Holy Spirit is drawing them more into his kingdom. Interestingly enough, in the process of attempting to do this, good, healthy boundaries are created. If someone is not interested in engaging relationally, or actively pursuing God's kingdom, or just wants their church fix for the week, we are not really offended if they don't stick around. On the other hand, we must learn to develop what the Scriptures define as long-suffering with each other who are sticking with the process. That is not fun or exciting from a cultural perspective, but the community that is created as a by-product is pretty earth-shattering on its own.

What Is Church?

A Theology of Fun, True Discipleship, and Simplicity

Here's a quote from an article I wrote a few years ago:

People will come from east and west and north and south, and will take their places at the feast in the kingdom of God." (Luke 13.29) Jesus often used the party or feast to represent the kingdom of God. His first miracle was performed at a wedding reception, he feasted with his brand new followers Levi and Zacchaeus, and his most famous parable ended with a huge party for a prodigal son. Often, Christians think true spirituality looks more like fasting than it does feasting. But Jesus responds, "Do wedding guests fast while celebrating with the groom? (Luke 5.34)

The next aspect of our ethos is what I am beginning to call *A Theology of Fun*. For many of us, our formation in church has led us to believe that the Holy Spirit only works during serious times—preaching, sharing, prayer, reading of scripture, singing thoughtful songs, during silence. This reality has created an unhelpful dualism which encourages people to be spiritual during sacred times and *normal* everywhere else. However, it has been our experience that some of the most powerful, formational moments can happen in the most benign settings—at the dinner table with friends, on the back porch with the guys, or at the grocery store. This is not to neglect the more serious moments, but rather to fill the times, where our guard is down, with the same desire for God's kingdom as during an intimate time of praise.

Playing together, eating together, laughing together—this is all serious business in the kingdom of God. We are representing something powerfully countercultural—a group of adults and our children, not just wasting our time or drowning our sorrows, but demonstrating that our productivity is not the most important thing, our financial or social status does not matter, and our relationship to one another is based on something more than we have the same hobby or like the same sports team. We are a forgiven people. We are a loved people. That is truly a sensational thing, and something we should celebrate often.

Along these lines is the recognition that simply engaging in church-related activities does not make someone a disciple. For far too long, churches have used attendance at services or bible studies to be a thermometer of growth or maturity. However, over the years our community has come back again and again to the reality that the only worthwhile measuring stick for discipleship is how we are adhering to the teachings of Jesus and the Scriptures in all of our choices and interactions. In other words, there is more to following Jesus than showing up at church. Instead of being the means to discipleship, our times together serve to help one another interpret how Jesus is teaching us in our day-to-day lives.

For this reason, it is natural to assume that a central part of our ethos would be simplicity in all things. Simplicity means that we will not allow ourselves to be so immersed in church activities or church relationships that we are unable to be present to what God is doing in our neighborhoods, jobs, schools, or even families. This requires some discipline on our part—sometimes we have to say *no* to each other and make difficult decisions about our time. Also, we have to understand that our needs are not always going to be met immediately and not everyone will be able to attend everything that the group plans. But simplicity has some deeper implications that will challenge—if we allow it to —some of our deepest held assumptions about how church is supposed to work in some traditionally controversial areas.

What Is Church?

Leadership, Structure, and Mission

Over the past five or six years, the most controversial questions that I and others around me have wrestled with typically fall under one of these five subjects: leadership, structure, mission, commitment, or money. They are the proverbial tail that wags the dog when it comes to people rediscovering what it means to be the church in our day and age. There has been so much ink spilled and breath wasted on these topics that I almost want to cut this chapter short and say, "That's enough for now!" However, I want to reiterate that all of this is written from a local perspective and requires some unpacking for those of us journeying together.

Earlier I said, "We can no longer just sit around and learn about what Jesus said, or debate his words, or just put them into nice worship songs. The Way of Jesus must be attempted or it is not a Way at all." This aspect of our ethos is the hinge point on which all the other aspects either succeed or fail. Either we follow Jesus—the intelligent, passionate, holy, loving, alive Jesus—or we follow Jesus the icon, the ideal, or the idol. If we follow the *real* Jesus, he has a habit of reorganizing our priorities around his, which are not easily managed. If we are to believe C.S. Lewis, "Jesus is not safe...but he is good."

The simplicity of following Jesus causes us to reorder what we think is important about church and the Christian life. How important is leadership, structure, commitment, or money? For some, they are what makes church, church. "Without vision, my people perish!" is the leadership slogan. What happens during the Sunday morning meeting has probably split more churches and denominations than anyone would care to admit. Defining who is *in* and who is *out* could almost qualify as the national pastime among

Christians. And do I even need to say anything about money? Money is, next to theological differences, the most divisive force among Christians around the world today. Truly, nothing new is under the sun.

I can attest to the fact that a healthy, loving, caring, and passionate community of Christians can exist without making these subjects primary concerns. In fact, I will argue (again, not to convince anyone, but rather to simply report on what I have seen and experienced) that if these subjects are of secondary importance, they find their rightful home within the church and among followers of Jesus.

Leadership happens within our community in a myriad of different ways and forms. Attempting to assign *leader* and *follower* labels to people at this point would be absurd. If anything, in the New Testament, all the titles we typically think synonymous with leadership are most always associated with sacrificial acts of service. When leadership happens, it is to the end of serving the community, of giving oneself for the betterment of others. The person leading in that instance does not expect anything in return—power, title, status, or even a pat on the back. It's all about the community, stupid.

But, you may ask, what about complex issues such as authority or church discipline? Of course, things are never neat and clean when there are sinners involved, which would include all of us. Again, that is why leadership exists as a service to the community as directed and empowered by the Holy Spirit, not through our own structures or abilities. Authority is expressed by the Spirit through a community committed to maturity in Christ. Although we are sinners, we are not children, and just as God has commissioned us to lead our families and look for the Spirit's guidance in all our family affairs, so we are to do the same for one another.

Likewise, the structure of church has become way too

important in the minds of many Christians, particularly leaders. How one *does church* is supposedly a pathway to understanding the genetic code, the DNA if you will, of a faith community. Judging a church's quality of life within, depth of relationship, or passion for God's kingdom by analyzing how a church organizes their gatherings is a dangerous path to tread.

In our community, we have always attempted to place our gatherings in their proper context. Let me give an example. One of my favorite analogies about our community is that when we gather, it is like attending a family reunion. There are some at the reunion who you see on a regular basis—brothers, sisters, moms, and dads. There are others you see less occasionally, but are still your family—great aunts and second cousins. Food is served, stories are told, music is played, the old (great-granddaddy and grandmama) and the weak (the newborns and rambunctious three year olds) are honored. There are laughter, arguments, and serious talks about serious family business. But at the center of this gathering is the fact that you are one family. Imagine if you were to wander uninvited into someone's family reunion and heard an argument or a terse conversation. Or you saw Uncle Billy over in the corner having one too many beers. Does that disqualify a family from being a family? Of course not, because we all live with the realities of sin within our own families, yet we still belong.

This is church-family. This is Peter and Paul having a *sharp disagreement* and parting ways, or Paul opposing Peter "to his face, because he was clearly in the wrong" (Galatians 2.11). These were the patriarchs of the first Christian family, not getting along like nice boys should. However, this is the stuff of real family, or—dare I say it—authentic community. Structure is always subject to these raw, organic family interactions.

There is some necessary structure to support family. However, it does not have to be all that complicated and certainly should be nothing anyone frets about too much. Imagine church structure as an *upside-down umbrella*. Instead of attempting to create an infrastructure capable of covering an array of ministries, programs, and initiatives, why not turn the umbrella upside-down so it serves people, rather than people serving it?

Structure and leadership among disciples of Jesus are not tasks to be farmed out to professionals. They are also not to be ignored. As I discussed in Chapter 6, our community has been profoundly influenced by the example of Alcoholics Anonymous as a structure to (in their words) stay focused on a primary purpose. For A.A. that purpose is to keep carrying its message to the alcoholic that still suffers. For us, it is carrying the message of God's kingdom and all it entails to both addict and otherwise, to those who *have it all* and those who have nothing. Like A.A, only a simple skeleton is necessary to keep redirecting us back to our primary purpose.

Creating this skeleton is a leadership task, but it is not intended to require constant babysitting once it is created. The purpose is to shape an environment where people are first free and able to dream, then able to pursue those dreams with the full support of the community behind them. This involves training for servant leadership, theological acumen, and experience in the ways of spiritual formation.

Of course, all of this leads to mission, which is birthed by God for his purposes. He calls us into places of pain to which we as the church bear together. There are countless books being written about mission and church right now and I do not wish to add to the complexity of the discussion. In fact, I want to suggest that being *missional* is both simpler and more complex than we have been led to believe. Simpler, because mission is born from the heart of God and is endowed to his people as he chooses. But infinitely more complex because of the deep humility and patience that is required to follow God's leading.

There is a beauty and mystery in watching someone move from brokenness to healing, to being released into the world as an agent of God's kingdom. So much of the conversation about what it means to be missional destroys this mystery. Who can predict how God will lead someone? Who are we to judge someone's activities as not missional enough? What if in the mind of God, a mother serving her young children is as missional as someone helping a thousand homeless people? We have found in our community that each individual undergoes a unique process that requires unique support and encouragement. There is no way around this. As much as we enjoy pontificating about the missional church and its identity, we are individuals with unique callings. Some of us will be called together for a time for a particular purpose. For some, a calling can become a lifelong vocation. For others, they need to see how even in the ordinary they have the opportunity to be ambassadors of God's kingdom. Mission is not another initiative for the church to master. It is rather a natural part of being an apprentice of Jesus that the whole community must be aware of and take ownership.

Commitment and Money

Starting sometime around the 1950s, there began a considerable amount of hand-wringing regarding what it meant to be a member of a church. Before that time, folks just assumed if you said you were a Methodist or a Baptist, your name was on the membership roll of a local church and you participated in that church's activities. However, during the cultural explosion that took place after World War II, people began to understand that they had options as consumers. They were no longer tied to what their family did or the expectations of their neighborhood. The suburbs created brand new opportunities to play the religious field, and this attitude naturally led pastors and leaders into the Church Growth movement of the '80s and '90s. In many ways, church membership these days looks more like brand loyalty than it does a conscious engagement with a group of people.

One response to this situation has been to clearly define the parameters for who is *in* or *out* of an organization. This can be done by encouraging allegiance to a leader, various doctrinal stances, or traditions. Another path has been to establish a step-by-step pathway for someone to move from an *attender* to a full-fledged participant in the organization's vision and mission. But where these methods have been successful in attaching consumers to particular organizations, have they addressed the deeper question of how someone becomes a true disciple of Jesus among other disciples? It should be obvious that in the context of a faith community, commitment should mean more than you have taken the required classes, can recite the right dogma, or have bought enough of the pastor's books and tapes.

Over the years, our community has at various times reestablished that the primary rallying point for what it means to be *committed* is to declare, "I want to be (and continue to learn how to grow as) an apprentice of Jesus." What this has meant, in short, is to intend to live a Jesus kind of life, as if he were we. This is not a side project, Sunday-morning-best kind of spirituality. This is full-body Christianity; no holds barred wrestling with God about every detail of our sinful in-need-of-redemption lives. It also means that we are forced to deal with each other as we really are, not just how we would like to present ourselves at a worship service. This, of course, is a scary prospect, and not one entered into lightly. If this commitment cannot be made for whatever reason, there are no hard feelings or ill wishes. If it takes someone years to make a decision to pursue Jesus in community, that is perfectly acceptable from the community's point of view. However, it has been our experience that over time an atmosphere is created where people voluntarily give their love and allegiance to one another. In this atmosphere, it becomes natural (or at least possible) to bear one another's burdens, rejoice in each other's triumphs, and grow in deeper obedience and passion for Jesus.

Of course, one of the areas affected by apprenticing yourself to Jesus is how you deal with money. Building on the entire ethos as I've described it up until this point, it should be obvious that we probably look at money a little differently than what is stereotypical for the church. First of all, money is not a tool God uses to beat us into submission. We have rejected the idea that the church needs money to function, for us to be what God intends us to be in the world. Rather, we have been captured by the reality (and promise) that the full resources of God's kingdom are at our fingertips—both monetarily and otherwise. As Americans we believe that our money is a pretty powerful thing, but as Christians we should see that our money is about as worthless as monopoly bills compared to God's resources. That being said, we have seen that God can use even our pocket change to do some pretty amazing things—from sponsoring Compassion kids to helping out a single mom who is having trouble paying her mortgage. The goal is to detach ourselves from being too enamored with our money or stuff. As we are freed from those idolatries, we become free to serve financially in whatever way God sees fit and champion causes that otherwise become buried in our consumer culture.

An Ethos Continues

It is important to note that this is not the end of how our community will continue to change its definition. Every person we journey with as a companion will bring something to help redefine another facet. As raw and as ugly as it seems at times, God has promised that he will make something beautiful. But as with anything beautiful, he does not promise that things will come quickly or easily. The hope for us as a church is not survival or longevity for its own sake, but rather *a long obedience in the same direction* as an aspect of our common apprenticeship to Jesus.

Epilogue

In the introduction, I said that this would not be a how-to or why book, but would seek instead to pose the question, "What if?" What if church could be a place for people to discover life as it was meant to be lived? What if following Jesus was the only priority worth having? What if the community that grew out of this common commitment to Jesus would be something subversive, healing, and sustainable? What if the kingdom of God comes through normal people, sacrificially giving themselves to one another, and trying to live out the teachings of Jesus among their friends and neighbors?

Could it be that simple?

Well, yes and no.

There are plenty of books being written right now

about doing church differently. The emerging church, missional church, simple church, the new monasticism, the new Reformed—all have their apologists. My hope in writing this book is to demonstrate that the reality of living out something *different* in the twenty-first century is a lot harder than it seems. Americans epitomize the seeds that fall on rocky soil in Jesus' parable: "Some fell on rocky places, where it did not have much soil. It sprang up quickly, because the soil was shallow" (Matthew 13.5). Church reform movements are like seeds on rocky soil. God has used them throughout history, because they do produce rapidly growing plants. But how many of those plants get swept away because they lack roots?

Growing roots requires good soil, nutrients, and time. None of what I have written in these pages will happen quickly. Are you willing to spend five, ten, twenty, or fifty years discovering the way forward? God is not alarmed by the state of the church nor its future. He is simply looking for people who will trust him and patiently allow his Spirit to grow them into something eternal.

On the Blue Ridge Parkway in North Carolina, there are *scenic overlooks* every few miles. They serve no other purpose than to give you space to stop and take in a little more of God's creation. For some, this book will have been like one of those scenic overlooks. Perhaps it made you stop and ask some new questions about following Jesus and church. You leave refreshed and go back to wherever you live, glad that there are places like this in the world. But others might have trouble leaving. Perhaps you are wondering why you have to leave. Why can't this be my home? It certainly won't be an easy place to live. There will not be many who want to come live with you.

This is my new home, for better or worse. The Apostle Paul spoke of building with gold, silver, and precious stones.

I don't imagine that kind of building happens quickly. The tools most valuable to building these missional communities provide no shortcuts. Like a jeweler, the slow, constant pressure of the Spirit draws us deeper into Jesus and his kingdom. Ultimately, the people involved in this process will be earmarked by persistence, intentionality, and suffering rather than an organizational skill-set.

In the movie, "The Shawshank Redemption," Andy Dufresne escapes prison using only a tiny sculpting tool. He did not use explosives or incite a riot. He did not decide to escape and then make a quick, unplanned attempt the next day. He also did not throw himself on the mercies of the parole board hoping (wishfully) to be released early. Instead, he chose a path that required the one thing he had plenty of—time. Patience is not a wimpy virtue, it is a subversive weapon. It can destroy enemies that seem overwhelmingly massive and strong, yet it will go undetected. If we are determined to find freedom and discover God's call individually and corporately, then we must determine to stick it out with Jesus for the long haul. Our prisons of addiction are more impenetrable than Alcatraz ever was. But as ones who are determining to submit our entire life to the kingdom of God, we have the advantage of time, each other, and the Creator of the Universe.

Endnotes

Introduction

1. Walter Brueggemann, *The Prophetic Imagination*, 2nd ed. (Minneapolis, MN: Fortress Press, 2001), 40.

Chapter One. Entering The Dream Of God

1. Dallas Willard, *The Divine Conspiracy: Rediscovering Our Hidden Life in God*, 1st ed. (San Francisco, CA: HarperSanFrancisco, 1998), 301.
2 Ibid., 25.
3. N. T. Wright, *The Challenge of Jesus: Rediscovering Who Jesus Was and Is* (Downers Grove, IL: InterVarsity Press, 1999), 37. The three most recognizable examples of these options were the zealots, Herod with the Romans, and the writers of the Dead Sea Scrolls (the Essenes).

What Is Church?

4. Ibid., 46.
5. Willard, *The Divine Conspiracy*, 27.
6. "Facts About the Video Industry," Available from http://www.
   idealink.org/Resource.phx/vsda/pressroom/quick-facts.htx
   (accessed June 13, 2008).
7. Wright, *The Challenge of Jesus*, 43.

Chapter Two. Detoxing From Church

1. Wendell Berry, *Jayber Crow: A Novel* (Washington, D.C.:
   Counterpoint, 2000).
2. Don Williams, *Jesus and Addiction: A Prescription to Transform the
   Dysfunctional Church and Recover Authentic Christianity*, 1st ed. (San
   Diego, CA: Recovery Publications, 1993).
3. Talking Heads, "Little Creatures: Road to Nowhere," (Warner
   Brothers, 1985).
4. Wright, *The Challenge of Jesus*, 36, 67. "When they [the Jews] longed
   for the kingdom of God, they were not thinking about how
   to secure themselves a place in heaven after they died. The
   phrase "kingdom of heaven," which we find frequently in
   Matthew's Gospel where the others have "kingdom of God,"
   does not refer to a place, called "heaven," where God's people
   will go after death. It refers to the rule of heaven, that is, of
   God, being brought to bear in the present world. Thy kingdom
   come, said Jesus, thy will be done, on earth as it is in heaven.
   Jesus' contemporaries knew that the creator God intended
   to bring justice and peace to his world here and now. The
   question was, how, when and through whom?"
5. Richard J. Foster, *Streams of Living Water: Celebrating the Great
   Traditions of Christian Faith*, 1st ed. (San Francisco, CA:
   HarperSanFrancisco, 1998), xv.
6. Foster's nomenclature for the streams, which he acknowledges
   is imperfect, are The Contemplative Tradition, or the
   prayer-filled life; The Holiness Tradition, or the virtuous
   life; The Charismatic Tradition, or the Spirit-empowered
   life; The Social Justice Tradition, or the compassionate life;
   The Evangelical Tradition, or the Word-centered life; The
   Incarnational Tradition, or the sacramental life.

Chapter Three. The Death Of A Pastor

1. Eugene H. Peterson, *The Contemplative Pastor: Returning to the Art of Spiritual Direction* (Grand Rapids, MI: William. B. Eerdmans Publishing Company, 1993), 58.
2. Darrell L. Guder and Lois Barrett, *Missional Church: A Vision for the Sending of the Church in North America* (Grand Rapids, MI: William B. Eerdmans Publishing Company, 1998), 195.
3. Ibid., 200.
4. Ibid., 195.
5. *Rev. Magazine* 2006
6. Greg Hawkins, "Willow Creek Repents," *Christianity Today.* Available from http://blog.christianitytoday.com/outofur/archives/2007/10/willow_creek_re.html (accessed June 13 2008). Quotes in this section taken from this article.
7. Ibid.
8. Paul Hemp, "Where Will We Find Tomorrow's Leaders," Available from http://harvardbusinessonline.hbsp.harvard.edu/hbsp/hbr/articles/article.jsp?articleID=R0801J&ml_action=get-article&print=true (accessed June 13 2008).

Chapter Four. The Failure Of Community

1. See www.allelon.org.
2. See www.vineyardcentral.com.
3. See www.landingplace.org.
4. Dietrich Bonhoeffer, *Life Together: The Classic Exploration of Faith in Community* (San Francisco, CA: HarperOne, 1978), 26-27.
5. Ibid., 28.
6. bid., 30.

Chapter Five. Christian Subversion

1. Brueggemann, *The Prophetic Imagination*, 46-47.
2. Ibid., 51.
3. Dallas Willard, *Renovation of the Heart: Putting on the Character of Christ*, Interactive student ed. (Colorado Springs, CO: NavPress, 2002), 15.

4. "Global Mission Trends," Joshua Project. Available from http://www.joshuaproject.net/assets/GlobalMissionTrendsMap.pdf (accessed June 13 2008). "In 2006, $24 billion was embezzled by church staff and treasurers world-wide. This is $2 billion more than the $22 billion world's annual giving to missions. Eliminating this fraudulent activity within the Church could add billions of dollars to global missions."
5. Peterson, *The Contemplative Pastor*, 34.
6. Wright, *The Challenge of Jesus*, 64.
7. Ibid., 85.
8. Joel Coen, "O Brother, Where Art Thou," (Touchstone Pictures).
9. Guder and Barrett, *Missional Church*, 160.
10. Ibid.
11. Rodney Clapp, *A Peculiar People: The Church as Culture in a Post-Christian Society* (Downers Grove, IL: InterVarsity Press, 1996), 100.
12. For more about Bob Ekblad and his story, see his website www.bobekblad.com.

Chapter Six. Apprentices Of Jesus

1. Willard, *The Divine Conspiracy*, 273.
2. Wright, *The Challenge of Jesus*, 54-55. "With symbols goes controversy. Tease someone about their nationality if you wish, provided you know them well and they are tolerant, but do not even think of burning their flag. Churchgoers are often quite tolerant of strange doctrines and even outlandish behavior from their clergy, but let the clergy try putting the church flowers in a different spot, and they will discover the power of symbols to arouse passion."
3. For more information about Al-Anon, visit http://www.al-anon.alateen.org.
4. Paula Polk Lillard and Lynn Lillard Jessen, *Montessori from the Start: The Child at Home from Birth to Age Three*, 1st ed. (New York, NY: Schocken Books, 2003), 3.
5. Ibid., 8.
6. Sofia Cavalletti, *The Religious Potential of the Child* (New York, NY: Paulist Press, 1983), 8.
7. C. Christopher Smith, *Water, Faith, and Wood: Stories of the Early Church's Witness for Today*, 1st ed. (Indianapolis, ID: Doulos Christou Press, 2003), 34.

What Is Church?

8. Ibid., 9.
9. Willard, *Renovation of the Heart*, 236-240.

Chapter Seven. The Jesus Underground

1. Rob Moll, "Great Leap Forward—China Is Changing and So Is Its Church. How New Urban Believers Are Shaping Society in Untold Ways," *Christianity Today*, May 2008.

Chapter Eight. Uncovering An Ethos

1. Wright, N. T. *Jesus and the Victory of God*. Minneapolis, MN: Fortress Press, 1996.
2. "Ethos," Dictionary.com. Available from http://dictionary. reference.com/browse/ethos (accessed June 13 2008).
3. Willard, *The Divine Conspiracy*, 314.
4. This was a favorite phrase of the founder of the Vineyard, John Wimber.

Bibliography

Berry, Wendell. *Jayber Crow: A Novel*. Washington, D.C.: Counterpoint, 2000.

Bonhoeffer, Dietrich. *Life Together: The Classic Exploration of Faith in Community*. San Francisco, CA: HarperOne, 1978.

Brueggemann, Walter. *The Prophetic Imagination*. 2nd ed. Minneapolis, MN: Fortress Press, 2001.

Cavalletti, Sofia. *The Religious Potential of the Child*. New York, NY: Paulist Press, 1983.

Clapp, Rodney. *A Peculiar People: The Church as Culture in a Post-Christian Society*. Downers Grove, IL: InterVarsity Press, 1996.

Coen, Joel. "O Brother, Where Art Thou." Touchstone Pictures.

"Ethos", Dictionary.com Available from http://dictionary. reference.com/browse/ethos (accessed June 13 2008).

"Global Mission Trends", Joshua Project Available from http:// www.joshuaproject.net/assets/GlobalMissionTrendsMap. pdf (accessed June 13 2008).

"Facts About the Video Industry" Available from http://www. idealink.org/Resource.phx/vsda/pressroom/quick-facts.htx (accessed June 13, 2008).

Foster, Richard J. *Streams of Living Water: Celebrating the Great Traditions of Christian Faith.* 1st ed. San Francisco, CA: HarperSanFrancisco, 1998.

Guder, Darrell L., and Lois Barrett. *Missional Church: A Vision for the Sending of the Church in North America.* Grand Rapids, MI: William B. Eerdmans Publishing Company, 1998.

Hawkins, Greg, "Willow Creek Repents," *Christianity Today* Available from http://blog.christianitytoday.com/outofur/ archives/2007/10/willow_creek_re.html (accessed June 13 2008).

Heads, Talking. "Little Creatures: Road to Nowhere." 4:19 minutes: Warner Brothers, 1985.

Hemp, Paul, "Where Will We Find Tomorrow's Leaders" Available from http://harvardbusinessonline.hbsp.harvard. edu/hbsp/hbr/articles/article.jsp?articleID=R0801J&ml_ action=get-article&print=true (accessed June 13 2008).

Lillard, Paula Polk, and Lynn Lillard Jessen. *Montessori from the Start: The Child at Home from Birth to Age Three.* 1st ed. New York, NY: Schocken Books, 2003.

Moll, Rob. "Great Leap Forward—China Is Changing and So Is Its Church. How New Urban Believers Are Shaping Society in Untold Ways." *Christianity Today*, May 2008.

Peterson, Eugene H. *The Contemplative Pastor: Returning to the Art of Spiritual Direction*. Grand Rapids, MI: William. B. Eerdmans Publishing Company, 1993.

Smith, C. Christopher. *Water, Faith, and Wood: Stories of the Early Church's Witness for Today*. 1st ed. Indianapolis, ID: Doulos Christou Press, 2003.

Rev. Magazine. September–October 2006.

Willard, Dallas. *The Divine Conspiracy: Rediscovering Our Hidden Life in God*. 1st ed. San Francisco, CA: HarperSanFrancisco, 1998.

_____. *Renovation of the Heart: Putting on the Character of Christ*. Interactive student ed. Colorado Springs, CO: NavPress, 2002.

Williams, Don. Jesus and Addiction: *A Prescription to Transform the Dysfunctional Church and Recover Authentic Christianity*. 1st ed. San Diego, CA: Recovery Publications, 1993.

Wright, N. T. *The Challenge of Jesus: Rediscovering Who Jesus Was and Is*. Downers Grove, IL: InterVarsity Press, 1999.

Printed in the United States
133951LV00002B/43/P